Critical Dimensions

The Art of Public Address Criticism

STUDIES IN *Speech*

Consulting Editor DON GEIGER

University of California, Berkeley

RANDOM HOUSE / *New York*

Critical Dimensions

The Art of Public Address Criticism

by ANTHONY HILLBRUNER

California State College at Los Angeles

To Laura

ACKNOWLEDGMENTS: *I am grateful to:*

Dr. Kenneth G. Hance of Michigan State University for first stimulating my thinking in the criticism of public address;

Dr. Don Geiger of the University of California at Berkeley for his aid in the formation of this book;

The California State College at Los Angeles Foundation for a small grant which enabled me to do some of the research necessary for this study.

Contents

Critical Dimensions

The Art of Public Address Criticism

Introduction

While criticism of public address has been going on since the first orator stood up to persuade his peers to take a certain course of action, it has only been in the last several decades that it has attained academic stature and prestige. Herbert A. Wichelns' precedent establishing "The Literary Criticism of Oratory" was an extremely persuasive document when it was published in 1925. It not only established the benchmarks which academic rhetorical critics tried to use in their own criticism, but it also set out the methodological process by which effective criticism was to be attained. In this work, Wichelns analyzed a number of analytical and critical approaches used by important literary critics. He found most of them wanting in what he, as a critic, would term "true" rhetorical criticism. He proposed a "full blown" critical approach. This was of great value to future generations of critics. It provided a rationale that rhetorical critics had been seeking; it provided a differentiation, a significant one, between literary and rhetorical evaluation. For all this, rhetorical scholars should be extremely grateful.

In a way, however, Wichelns has done the critic of public address a disservice with his emphasis upon a "full blown" criticism. The public address critic, after Wichelns, attempted to use *all* the rhetorical factors—or as many as were feasible within the manageable limits of the essay—to evaluate the speaker. Moreover, he tried to use these all the time. This is not to say that the critiques that have followed him are of no value; quite the contrary. At a time when much criticism was impressionistic, fragmentary, even capricious, Wichelns called for a disciplined scholarly approach. Unfortunately for public address criticism, he was too persuasive. In establishing criteria for speech scholars (most of the essays in the first two volumes of the *History and Criticism of American Public Address* were modeled after his formulations), he accomplished his purpose of rejuvenating public address criticism too well. In the process, therefore, his call for a definitive criticism also had its pernicious effects.

One effect was to force a pattern of criticism—largely the Aristotelian one—on speech scholars, thereby hampering the latent creativity of a diversity of approaches to criticism. Another was the emphasis upon the "full blown" approach. A third fostered an almost unnatural objectivity on critics, restricting their intuitive discernments and their use of critical assessments.

It is only now that public address critics are breaking out of the rhetorical cocoon that was so strongly wound about them by Wichelns. Some of the creativity and diversity in criticism which had been present before Wichelns, even though it was undisciplined then, are returning to effective rhetorical assessment. In other words, criticism after Wichelns had attained unity but began to lack variety. The unified approach needed to be recommended, since speech research and criticism in the academic community was in its infancy, had little standing and therefore needed to be prodded. This Wichelns accomplished most admirably.

Yet, despite Wichelns, when one examines the criticism of public address one can find some diversity, much of which has appeared within the last decade or so. Contemporary critics are beginning to follow the conception that useful evaluation can have as its aim the criticism of almost any significant aspect of public address. It can concern itself with a speech: its ideas or its artistry or lack of either; its impact; its relation to current intellectual, scientific, religious, political, philosophical, educational or artistic problems; its relation to the speaker's deeds; its value; its results. Criticism can concern itself with a speaker in a "full blown" way, and this can be done on different levels. It can describe the circumstances of a speaker's life; it can analyze and interpret these circumstances; and finally, it can evaluate them in some meaningful way.

That there is no one critical approach to speaker, speech, and audience has now been accepted. Art is long. It has manifold ramifications. And certainly no small volume can deal fully with all of them.

This book's purpose is to select a number of rhetorical critical approaches, examine their underlying bases and objectives, illustrate the approaches with excerpts from essays and monographs, ask questions about them, analyze and assess their value, and suggest problems for further work and study. In short, this is an analysis of criticism. It is all related to two fundamental questions. *How* good is contemporary criticism of public address? *What* good is contemporary criticism of public address? Hopefully, the student of public address, who may eventually burgeon as a rhetorical critic, will gain from this examination a discernment into the criticism of public address.

This work is organized in two parts: the first part will be concerned with the extrinsic factors in criticism; the second will focus on the intrinsic ones.

The extrinsic factors are those exterior to the speech itself, although of salient significance to it. They are such factors as the historical description and analysis of the times, of the audience and of the occasion. They deal with biographical description and analysis. And finally, they are concerned with a historical description and analysis of the effects of the speech.

The intrinsic factors are those dealing more comprehensively with the speech itself. They focus on a description and an analysis of the speaker's ideas, content, or invention, as well as with an interpretation and evaluation of them. Then, too, intrinsic factors are concerned with the more formal aspects of the speechmaking: structure, style, presentation. Here, of course, is rhetorical description and analysis as well as interpretation and evaluation of these important aspects of form. The latter two facets are especially significant primarily because of the comparative dearth of these in contemporary criticism.

The fact is, when one begins to study criticism of public address, one is amazed at the lack of emphasis on evaluation and comparative judgment. It could be that the focus on objective processes in criticism has brought this about. At any rate, most of the so-called criticism today really is historical scholarship. Some of it is descriptive and analytical, but little is actually critical in the more exact sense of the word as evaluative judgment. It is hoped that this book may suggest ways and means for effective valuation and thus give impetus to this phase of criticism.

In this work the study and evaluation of criticism, while it can be categorized in many different ways, will be concerned primarily with critical studies of speakers. Thus there will be no evaluation of such interesting approaches to public address and critical studies as the study of a significant period in speechmaking, such as the so-called "Golden Age of American Oratory." Nor will there be the study of an interesting area in which oratory bloomed, such as "Southern Oratory." Nor for that matter will it focus on a political or social movement related to oratory as "The Speaking of the Neo-Conservatives," or "The Populist Movement."

One must be aware that useful criticism—in the broad sense of the term—can even encompass the effective use of any one facet of the procedures suggested above. Description and analysis of the period, of the audience and occasion; description, analysis, interpretation and evaluation of specific canons and of the speaker himself—all constitute a legitimate kind of critical activity, always provided that it offers useful critical insights into some phase of public address. It is to that aim that this work is dedicated.

Part One.

Extrinsic Factors in the Criticism of Public Address

1 Historical Description and Analysis of the Times

Perhaps more than in the criticism of any art form, more than in literature, painting, or music, for instance, the times, or to put it more elaborately, the socio-cultural milieu, plays a significantly influential and molding role in public address and its criticism.

The importance of the social context for public address is omnipresent. In order to find the "essence" of a work of art such as a great speech, one must investigate the relation of the speaker's words to the civilization or culture that produced them.

That no speech is made in a vacuum is a truism in public address study. To be more explicit, every speech, especially a significant one, not only is the invention of the speaker, but a product of the time, the occasion, and the audience. Although a speech is given or produced by an individual, it really is a function of all these elements. Without them, and without a unique synthesis of them, no important speech could be given.

The critic's first job in his study of a specific speech, a group of speeches, or of a speaker, for that matter, is to discover what was happening at the juncture of history in which the speech event took place. The critic takes this segment of time, puts boundaries around it, isolates it, so to speak, by figuratively putting it under a microscope. After the examination, he notes the salient features of the period and describes its notable characteristics. For this, of course, he must rely upon his colleagues in such academic disciplines as history, economics, political science, and sociology. Much of this material, therefore, comes from secondary sources. In certain instances, however, such as in local or regional situations, the critic may find it necessary to go to original sources. This may be more difficult, but it is necessary.

In order to uncover the contextual background of the speech or the speaker, the critic must develop a keen historical sense for the data. He will be aided in his task if he relies on the great historians whenever feasible. This is so because it is historical discernment which the critic needs, and it is this insight which characterizes the great historical scholar.

Perhaps the simplest approach to the description of the times is to delineate the political situation. This is needful since American society is noted for the flux in which it often operates. Within the span of a decade, or a generation, for instance, the political picture nationally, or regionally, can be altered radically. Moreover, the change in political administrations, such as that from Herbert Hoover's *laissez-faire* Republican one to Franklin D. Roosevelt's New Deal Democratic one, often can be a significant index to the times. Such a substitution of administrations reflects the changing attitudes not only toward political questions and problems, but toward economic and social ones as well, since the latter two are inextricably tied to the former.

From this ever-changing political, economic and social construct comes the basic intellectual ingredients of the society. And from this comes something which is at once broader in one sense, and more specific in another. This is the value system.

Political theorists and sociologists tell us that the value system changes with the times. These changes, in the narrow sense, mean the interpretation of basic ideas (or values) of a specific society. The basic values themselves are not done away with very rapidly, however.

For example, an important basic idea in America is the democratic spirit, which is so often invoked by political, religious or social speakers. The three parts of this significant value are those virtues of a democratic society popularized in late 18th century France, *liberté, egalité,* and *fraternité*. They are still considered, especially the first two, as inalienable, natural rights.

In fact, one could say that the commitment of the great majority of Americans to the over-all value of democracy —that broad, nebulous term—has remained constant, strong, and unshakeable through the years. The value of the more specific ideas, however, which develop and support the broad one of democracy, such values as liberty, equality, and brotherhood, are constantly being altered in one way or another as time goes on.

Liberty, for example, has been considerably modified over the years, as has equality. No longer is liberty the *carte blanche* that it has been in the past, at least according to the ultra-conservative view. Much of the change in the functioning character of complete liberty has come about because of the force and potency of equality. The Negro's quest for a larger measure of equality in the civil, economic, political, and social sphere has been moderately successful. The pressures for equality by this large and important segment of society has meant that the liberty of restaurant owners, for example, to serve or not to serve the members of this minority group has been inhibited. It has meant, too, that the liberty of many white parents to send their children to all white public schools has ended. Their liberty has been modified. But the liberty of the Negro, as a result of the implementation of egalitarian ideals, has been enhanced.

Changes in the functioning implementation of certain ideas, such as liberty, are made when the pressure from another idea, such as equality, propounded by a segment of society, become great, almost overwhelming. In the past these pressures have led even to revolution. To weaken and eventually eliminate this revolutionary impulse, laws are made. The values of the society as a whole (there is little doubt of this) are changed by the laws, if not immediately, inevitably. However, just because the Civil Rights Bill with its accommodations for the Negroes was passed did not mean that the white southerner, or northerner, for that matter, now looked at the colored man as equal to himself.

The laws may require the whites to accommodate the

Negroes in the labor market, in eating establishments and in other ways in the South and the North. It does not mean, however, that the white man's attitude as part of the value system of his region will undergo an immediate metamorphosis. Nevertheless, there will be a slight change in the values that the society holds dear, since these ideas are being modified in the working and living sphere by the laws that are passed.

The public address critic, therefore, must take cognizance of stresses and strains in society before he can deal with the essential qualities of the speech and speaker.

The critic must be aware of the above factors because man is a growing and developing organism. As such he is affected in some way by the political and social conditions of his time. It does not mean that man will necessarily humbly acquiesce to these conditions—although he might. On the other hand, he may become an even more vigorous fighter for the values he held dear before they were altered by law.

As conditions change, the means for maintaining values are also changed. Some may have been taken away. Others may have been added. The means used depend quite naturally on the political and social complexion of the speaker and his view of the lawful modifications.

Instances are readily available. Some materials and tools to fight integration have been taken away from Governor George Wallace of Alabama and his segregationist peers. On the other hand, some materials and tools have been given to Dr. Martin Luther King, Jr. and his co-workers in the fight against discrimination.

Speakers are affected in different ways by the political situation, which in the long run can change the social complexion and, hence, the social values of a society. All this means is that more effective discernments into an understanding of the speaker can come about by a careful study and analysis of the times. Criticism of speech and speaker cannot help but be affected and perhaps enhanced by these considerations.

In addition to the social construct, which wields such pervasive influence, there is also the intellectual milieu.

This must also be examined and analyzed if full comprehension of the speaker is desired.

It is in this realm that the social and intellectual historians are so useful to the public address critic. The development of the histories of ideas, as histories go, is of rather recent vintage. It began with such pioneer scholars of the late 1800s as Moses Coit Taylor and his *The Literary History of the American Revolution*. It is interesting to note, also, that Taylor concerned himself with oratory as part of the general literature of the time. His primary focus, however, was on the speaking and writing of the main literary, religious, and political figures of the colonies. In this study of the "elite" spokesmen he investigated the questions of style as well as that of content. This meant that Taylor was a pioneer in the history of American literature and the history of ideas.

James Harvey Robinson's *The New History* and Charles Beard's *An Economic Interpretation of the Constitution* continued this development. Robinson was a reformist historian of ideas, who celebrated the power of human thought. But he also placed emphasis upon the power of the non-intellectual environment to mold ideas. He hoped that if the historian had a better understanding of the physical, economic, psychological and social forces in the environment, these would help him understand the formation of human thought. Beard, of course, further developed this view that thought is formed by social environmental influences. These early historians dealt with facets of the socio-intellectual tradition.

The first attempt to cover virtually the entire chronological sweep of American ideas was made by Vernon Louis Parrington. His *Main Currents in American Thought* was considered the "most preferred" American history published between 1920 and 1935. While the three volumes of this work resembled those of Moses Coit Taylor, James Harvey Robinson and Charles Beard, they formed a more distinguished American history of ideas than those of his predecessors. But Parrington did not concern himself with ideas in a single unified manner. Those ideas that he did not like he claimed came from environmental sources; those he favored, on the other hand, seemed to him to have an intellectual autonomy that the others did not.

A generation later Merle Curti followed in that tradition with his *The Growth of American Thought*. Curti's work illustrates his reformist social philosophy, his conception of the role of ideas in history and the breadth of his interests. He stressed the importance of pacifism and the traditional American humane values. His greatest emphasis, however, is similar to the earlier intellectual and social historians in that he gave a great deal of credence to social environment in forming ideas. He tried to describe the ideas themselves as well as the environment from which they came. His method, therefore, described the functional nature of intellectual activities rather than their interior nature.

This listing is herein delineated for two reasons. The first is the obvious one: that the reading of these books will provide insights into the ideological motivations of Americans. The second is perhaps less obvious. It is that in some cases the studies illustrate the possible environmental determinants that operate in society as well.

This should not mean, however, that the public address critic will rely on these, or like studies, completely. Perhaps the contrary should be the case. Each of the historians has his blind spots, his intellectual crotchets, his prejudices, if you will. The patterns of historical discovery, however, that these scholars have set are worthy of emulation if we want to comprehend the intellectual currents within which speakers had to operate. If we are to understand and criticize a speaker, we must discern his relationship to the times.

Even on this rather simple descriptive level of the handling of different historical materials there are problems of research. The main ones are the twin bugaboos which have plagued historians and rhetoricians alike: the problems of objectivity and subjectivity.

While many historians like to think of themselves as social scientists who are objective in historical method and procedure, very few, if any, succeed. The difficulty for the historian is similar to that of the public address critic and to the speaker himself. It is that all these—scholar, critic, and speaker—operate more in the realm of probability of public affairs than in the relative certainty of the scientist. Thus many historians—and rhetoricians as well—would probably agree with Arthur M. Schlesinger, Jr., who said that history is partly a matter of personal vision, and interpretation varies from historian to historian and generation to generation. One need only to read the works suggested above to see this subjective factor operative. From Moses Coit Taylor to Henry Steele Commager one finds special personal axes ground. One also finds specific social, intellectual, cultural, and political attitudes and assumptions operating. Many of these are undergirding for the subjective interpretations made.

Perhaps not too much can be done about trying to reach the acme of objectivity. Perhaps some subjectivity may be a good thing. In fact, the public address critic, if he has any talent at all, will not be too bound by the so-called objective analyses and critiques of his predecessors. If he were, the last word on many of the great speakers in America, from Jonathan Edwards to Franklin D. Roosevelt, will have been said.

It is the duty of the critic, however, to be as objective as possible in analyzing historical evidence for the purpose of evaluating a speaker. This very awareness and objective stance, while not completely fulfilling the aim of objectivity, will go some way toward attaining it. The critic, fallible and subjective as he often is, must constantly strive for at least a modicum of objectivity. He must use the criteria of the logician to check the particular historian's credentials. If the critic accepts a historian as an expert witness, which, of course, he is doing when he relies upon him, he must learn if the historian's analyses and interpretation are acceptable to a majority of historians. Consistency in internal evidence must be present and congruent with whatever other factual data is available. The critic must then use his own judgment based upon these and other factors before accepting or rejecting the historian's conclusions.

The problem of selectivity is allied to that of objectivity.

How is the critic of public address to ascertain what to use and what to reject of the historical materials gathered for his own study? How, in fact, is he to determine what are the best choices?

If the critic has followed the earlier injunctions, then by the process of elimination, based upon logical criteria, he has discarded the works of some of the historians as not suited to his purpose. He still may have a plethora of material, however, from which to choose. What then?

Here selectivity enters the picture. Moreover, while the critic will continue to sift and weigh, to cogitate and consider, all the while trying to be as detached as he can, there comes a moment when the ultimate decision is to be made. It is then that the critic should rely upon his extralogical perception. This is the composite of data and materials, uniquely synthesized in one's own mind, which has been called intuition. The critic may not know exactly why he selects from among several studies, but he feels that one of these finally is the right choice.

The critic must be careful, of course. But there is no reason why a critic should not trust his intuitive qualities when making choices, provided always that an impersonal procedure of analysis has first been followed. After all, this is done in life and in art. Moreover, public address criticism, as an art form, must have some of this intuitive knowledge, if it is to remain vigorous and creative. Too long has this art form suffered from a flaccid and passive pseudo-scientific objectivity. A leap of the mind, combining the best elements of rational and intuitive cognition, can be of great aid in keeping public address criticism at a high artistic level.

Many of these injunctions obviously transcend the descriptive level and lead naturally to the analytical and interpretative one. One important purpose in analyzing purely historical descriptive materials is to find the causes of certain historical events. Thus the critic, in analyzing the times for their impact upon the speaker, goes beyond the factual data and looks for causation. Here again his training in logic, in reasoning and inference should be useful.

Naturally, effects are more easily determined than

causes. One can examine the past to ascertain the result of a certain policy. But to seek the cause of a specific act is more difficult. For example, a scholar could ask himself the question: What caused the Civil War? He will, of course, come up with a number of different answers. Many of these would reflect the attitude and personal vision of a particular historian.

The early simplistic version of attributing the cause of the Civil War to the orators and propagandists of the South and North is now outdated. No longer do the speakers of the ante-bellum South, such as John C. Calhoun and William Yancey, or those of the North, such as Wendell Phillips and William Lloyd Garrison, have the historical causal influence they once had.

Later causal versions blamed economic determinism, or cultural and social differences. Then there developed the two nations theory: that the South and North were actually two different governmental states trying to live as one. While the rhetorical critic's difficulties are perhaps not as large as the question of the causes of the Civil War, they are, nevertheless, of similar significance.

The critic of public address, in trying to comprehend the events within a certain segment of time, will first draw inferences from a number of sources. Then, by dint of his own rhetorico-historical vision, he can make certain interpretations.

Interpretations, like inferences, come from the data explored. Facts do not speak for themselves. It is naive to accept still this early 19th century concept of the omnipotence of factual data. Frances Wright, vigorous woman orator of the "Age of the Common Man," exemplifies this romantic tradition. The prime role of education, she asserted in many hard-hitting speeches from the public platform and in editorials in the *Free Enquirer,* was to disseminate factual knowledge. After being given this information, the people would reach what Wright termed the "right" conclusions. They would make the "correct" judgments. This is patently not true. Evidence is only one part of the logical process; reasoning is another. Moreover, the very act of selection of factual data is, in a way, an act of analysis if not of interpretation.

It is the reasoning process which allows one to make *any* conclusions.

A notable example of interpretation in the field of rhetorical theory is the resurgence of interest in the enthymeme—in its role and function in rhetoric. James J. McBurney's pioneering study has been re-assessed by present day scholars and found to be incomplete. Some of the most recent of these studies, those of Charles Mudd and Lloyd Bitzer (both in the *Quarterly Journal of Speech*), have given different interpretations. These, if not contrary to traditional ideas of the enthymeme, differ on certain salient aspects of the role of the enthymeme in rhetoric.

How did this come about? The simplest answer would be that rhetorical theory, like history, has its revisionists. In fact, rhetoric should have them if it is to stay healthy and vigorous, and grow as an effective instrument of contemporary democratic society. Each generation interprets its history in accordance with its own attitudes and values. So too should it be with rhetorical theory, the history of public address, and public address criticism. Just because a history of the United States has been written does not mean that it is now the definitive one. Just because an analysis and criticism of a great speaker, speech, or epoch in speaking has been written does not mean, either, that it is the definitive one, that no others are needed. Whenever writers and critics begin with different starting points, different philosophies, different views of the world, their interpretations will necessarily differ. As a matter of fact, they should be different if there are to be new discernments into rhetorical theory and public address.

If rhetorical scholars and public address critics accept this idea, then new interpretations are constantly needful. It does not mean that these should be done on the basis of sketchy, inadequate or insufficient evidence. Sound and thorough research is necessary. Some of our prominent scholars have successfully accomplished this task and built their academic reputations upon such work.

Richard Hofstadter is a distinguished example. He became known to the academic community by his discerning interpretations of such well known figures as Thomas Jefferson, Andrew Jackson, John C. Calhoun, and Abraham Lincoln in his *The American Political Tradition and Its Makers*. In short but succinct summaries that sparkled with salient judgments, he corrected what he believed to be some misinterpretations about these figures. His interpetations are not romantic, naive, parochial, or chauvinistic. Instead, basing his analyses on newly discovered historical evidence and some reinterpretations of the old, Hofstadter gives us more realistic versions of the significant thought, character, and actions of some of the key figures of the American political and social scene. The myth of Lincoln's difficult struggle to the top of his profession, the myth of constant defeats, is exploded by Hofstadter. Instead, Hofstadter points out from the factual record a great amount of success. He points out that Lincoln, from the time he was 25 years old to the time of his death, except for two short intervals, was not only involved in politics, but most of the time successfully.

Hofstadter's *The Age of Reform* examines the passion for reform and progress that was the key to the period from 1890 to 1940. Hofstadter's aim here as a political historian was different from those of his predecessors. Instead of looking at old political platforms and long dead issues, Hofstadter took a psychological and rhetorical approach. He dissects the emotional drives and motives of the reformers; he delineates their dreams, social drives, and values, and compares these with the realities of their times. As a result, his analysis is fresh and fruitful; his interpretations valuable. Critics of public address and rhetoricians sometimes do the same. In fact, what Hofstadter the historian is doing to some degree is stealing the thunder of the rhetoricians for his historical contributions.

Of course the public address critic's aim is not the same as Hofstadter's. Rather the critic's role is to use the social construct only as a preliminary for understanding the speaker, a group of speakers, or an important period of oratory. Hence, his prime task is not to give new interpretations to historical data so much as it is to use the most discerning analyses as tools for rhetorical assessment. In other words, he will need to exercise his abilities as a critic even with historical materials.

Happily for the public address critic, he has effective starting points for understanding the times in which speakers operated. A good point is "The Historical Background of American Public Address," contained in Volume I of the *History and Criticism of American Public Address*. This is not merely a chronology of political administrations and events, although this can contribute to the tone for political oratory. Here also are analyses of the times, the ideas that were current and potent. Of necessity, somewhat simplified, since the three long essays attempt to indicate the total spectrum as a backdrop for the speakers who are analyzed in subsequent pages, the essays nevertheless point the way for further and deeper work. They also can serve as a necessary background. The following passage is illustrative of the qualities of the American mind in 1788, at the beginning of the Early National Period. Bower Aly and Grafton P. Tanquary point out that:

> Without respect to social status or location, some assumptions were held so generally in 1788 as to warrant their being used to characterize the national mind. The first of these was the assumption of perfectibility out of which apparently grew the prevailing buoyancy of spirit amid hardship and the belief in progress. The doctrine of progress was not a facile optimism. It was rather a basic attitude toward the value of struggling for a better time. . . .
>
> A second prevailing assumption was that kings and regal institutions are wicked in the nature of things. . . . The belief in democracy, however, was not widely held: fraternity and equality were matters of argument. . . .
>
> There was no argument on the question of liberty. The new French view of the rights of man merely served to confirm the old tradition of the rights of Englishmen. The American of 1788 believed in liberty, that is, his own liberty, with a passionate attachment difficult to describe. For the word *liberty* to him was not a semantic confusion. It was a symbol of concrete realities. It meant a freedom from every manner of restraint; a freedom to believe what he wished about God and to worship him or not as he

chose; a freedom to speak whatever he pleased, including profanity, without hindrance; a freedom to move about whenever he wished without interference by officers; a freedom from special assessment and, insofar as possible, from any taxes whatsoever. Not the least element of his concept of liberty was the freedom to hold property and to defend it against all comers.

A fourth and highly significant mental trait common to the people generally was an ethical equality relative not so much to questions of religion or personal morals—although such questions were often in the fore—as to the primary question of fair play or sportsmanship.[1]

It is not always enough, however, merely to indicate such political and social factors. These conditions should be related to the central object of a particular study. Aly and Tanquary accomplish this admirably in a pithy segment which shows just such a relationship. They say:

This ethical quality naturally is of the utmost importance to persuasion. If by unanimous consent a group has shared an agreement to arbitrate issues by persuasion rather than by other forms of force, the power of persuasion either in the written or spoken word is infinitely increased. If, however, persuasion is practiced in a social order where the resort to arms in the settling of questions has not been interdicted by an almost universal ethic, the art of persuasion may become simply the handmaiden—perhaps the concubine—of the warrior.[2]

Introductions by Ernest J. Wrage and Barnet Baskerville in their *American Forum* and *Contemporary Forum* are also successful delineations of the historical-social mode. In the following passage from their introduction to "Modernism vs. Fundamentalism in Religion," there can be seen how useful is the comprehension of the religious issues of the 1920's to the speaking on those issues by Harry Emerson Fosdick and William Jennings Bryan and John Gresham Machen. Wrage and Baskerville state:

The religious controversy between liberalism and orthodoxy after World War I furnishes striking parallels to the great controversy of a century before. Between 1815 and 1830, the Congregational Church of New England was

split by the Unitarian movement, and the "faith once delivered to the saints" was thrown on the defensive by the
heretical doctrines of William Ellery Channing, Ralph
Waldo Emerson, Theodore Parker, and others. In the 1920's
religious orthodoxy was once again threatened by innovations that called into question what had long been regarded
as eternal and unchanging truth. This time the attack came
from two directions: religious modernists, armed with the
higher criticism, discounted supernatural aspects of religion and disparaged Biblical literalism; and scientists
advanced an evolutionary hypothesis that seemed to con-
tradict the Biblical account of creation and therefore to
weaken faith in the infallibility of the Holy Scriptures.

This renewal of religious disputation was in some measure part of a general postwar reaction—the desire to return
to "normalcy" in religion as in other fields, a longing for
the old securities, and a resentment of experimentation,
innovation, and disturbing new ideas. Science had achieved
an immense prestige, and many devout Christians as-
sociated science with materialism, secularism and loss of
spiritual values. Believing that religious faith was being
undermined, they sought solace in orthodox creeds. Some
fundamentalists took refuge in unyielding obscurantism,
rejecting outright the discoveries of science whenever they
came into conflict with a literal interpretation of the Bible.
Modernists, on the other hand, wished to adopt Christian
principles to changing social conditions, and to reconcile
the new knowledge with the old faith.[3]

In the presentation of useful historical background, the
rhetorician and historian operate in similar ways. Here,
too, Richard Hofstadter makes a contribution in understanding the times as preludes to ideas and men. His two-
volume anthology, *Great Issues in American History*,
contains capsule descriptions of the significant events as
introductions to the documents themselves. Incidentally,
Hofstadter suggests the importance of speeches as important *documenta* of ideas by including the significant
excerpts from over forty speeches. He divides the time
span from the 18th century to our own time into important periods. Then he presents the historical events, tying
them in with the documents which are to follow. In this
way, he welds the two, historical data and specific docu-

ments, and in a reciprocal fashion, he thus sheds light on each. He says, for example, when considering the Jacksonian Era that:

A major issue during this period was the question of the proper role of the federal government in economic development. Most Americans seemed to prefer that such enterprises as the development of manufacturing and the building of a national network of roads and canals should be launched without central direction from the federal government. But political leaders such as Henry Clay and John Quincy Adams believed in a national plan that Clay called "the American System." They proposed to arrange sectional interests in a national harmony—the East should receive high tariffs to aid its manufacturers; the interior should get federally aided transportation to improve its access to market; and the agricultural sections should benefit from good roads and canals and the presence of domestic urban markets. John Quincy Adams went beyond these proposals. He hoped to enlist the federal government to also support science and education. His first annual message (Document 2), which proposed a national university and astronomic observatories, courageously expressed his belief that federal resources should be used in some general plan, but his views were received with obloquy and ridicule, and had much to do with his defeat in 1828. His successor, Andrew Jackson, checked but by no means stopped the movement for federal aid to internal improvements in his veto of the Maysville Road Bill (Document 3) in 1830. Since Jackson sometimes accepted and sometimes opposed such proposals, Henry Clay, whose project the bill was, twitted him for his inconsistency. Clay stated the general case for a system of internal improvements in a speech on "The American System" (Document 4) which he gave in answer to Jackson's veto.[4]

Vernon L. Parrington, the literary historian of ideas, also succeeds in presenting useful historical discernments in his epoch-making *Main Currents in American Thought*. As a scholar trained in literature rather than in history, his approach to historical description is quite different from that of the "pure" historians. His work is a gold mine for those interested not only in literature, but in government, history, and public address, and accomplishes two important objectives. These are an analytical inter-pretation of the times and a description, analysis, and interpretation of some of the important figures and their ideas as movers of those times. Taking the total intellec-tual spectrum as his bailiwick, he deals with speakers, writers, politicians, reformers, philosophers, statesmen, and others. But first he describes the historico-cultural milieu, as in the following on "The Colonial Mind:"

The undistinguished years of the early and middle eight-eenth century, rude and drab in their insularity, were the creative springtime of democratic America—plebeian years that sowed what after-times were to reap. The forgotten men and women of those silent decades wrote little, de-bated little, very likely thought little; they were plain workmen with whom ideas counted for less than the day's work. The stir of achievement filled the land, daily pene-trating farther into the backwoods and bringing new farm-lands under the plow. The stern demands of necessity held men in their grip, narrowing the horizon of their minds, and obscuring the vision of their larger accomplishment. Along the Appalachian watershed a vast drama, magnificent in the breadth and sweep of its movement, was being en-acted by players unconscious of their parts. Not until long after they had gone to their graves were the broad lines of that drama revealed. Today it is plain that those unremembered years were engaged in clearing away en-cumbrances more significant than the great oaks and maples of the virgin wilderness: they were uprooting ancient habits of thought, destroying social customs that had grown old and dignified in class-ridden Europe. A new psychology was being created by the wide spaces that was to be enormously significant when it came to self-con-sciousness. If this middle eighteenth century wrote little literature, it created and spread among a vigorous people something of far greater importance to America, the psychology of democratic individualism.

From this determining influence—too little recognized by later generations—the creative outlines of our history have taken shape. American ideals and institutions emerged in large part from the silent revolution which during the middle eighteenth century differentiated the American from the transplanted colonial; a change that resulted from an amalgam of the older English stock with other races, and the subjection of this new product on a great scale to the influence of diffused landholding. From these two major facts of a new race and a free environment came the social and political philosophy of older America, to which we have traditionally applied the term democratic, and which unconsciously wove itself into our daily intercourse and ways of thinking.[5]

Once Parrington has sketched in this general analysis of the work and thought of colonial times, he moves to a consideration of the two most important colonial figures: Jonathan Edwards and Benjamin Franklin. He interprets their thinking within this intellectual framework. Thus, one can see the reciprocity that exists between events and men when one looks at the following excerpts and relates them to Parrington's historical interpretation in the preceding passage. About Edwards he says:

There was both pathos and irony in the fate of Jonathan Edwards. . . . The greatest mind of New England had become an anachronism in a world that bred Benjamin Franklin. . . . The intellectual powers were his, but the inspiration was lacking; like Cotton Mather before him, he was the unconscious victim of a decadent ideal and petty environment. Cut off from fruitful intercourse with other thinkers, drawn away from the stimulating field of philosophy into the arid realm of theology, it was his fate to devote his noble gifts to the thankless task of reimprisoning the mind of New England within a system from which his nature and his powers summoned him to unshackle it. He was called to be a transcendental emancipator, but he remained a Calvinist.[6]

Consider now Parrington's concluding statement about Franklin. It indicates lucidly that Franklin had a completely different relationship to the times than did Edwards.

Franklin . . . was a part of that emerging humanitarian movement which, during the last half of the eighteenth century, was creating a new sense of social responsibility. True to his Physiocratic convictions, Franklin was socialminded. He was concerned not with property or class interests, but with the common welfare; and in his quick sympathy for all sorts and conditions of men, in his conviction that he must use his talents to make this world better and not exploit it, he reveals the breadth and generosity of his nature. Reason and work, in his pragmatic philosophy, are the faithful handmaids of progress, of which war, whether public or private, is the utter negation. . . .

. . . Franklin ended as he began, the child of a century marked by sharp spiritual limitations. What was best in that century he made his own. In his modesty, his willingness to compromise, his openmindedness, his clear and luminous understanding, his charity—above all, in his desire to subdue the ugly facts of society to some more rational scheme of things—he proved himself a great and useful man, one of the greatest and most useful whom America has produced.[7]

It cannot be over-emphasized that the student of public address who is interested in analysis and criticism of men and ideas must also be a student of history. He must have an abiding interest in historical, cultural, ideological, and intellectual events if he is to comprehend public address and its role in society, and if he is to make lasting critical contributions to his discipline.

QUESTIONS AND PROJECTS

1. Select one of the following areas in American civilization: history, philosophy, politics, religion, or reform. Then, using specific evidence to develop your ideas, write a short paper indicating the relationship of public address to one of these.
2. It has often been said by rhetoricians that speakers have been exemplars or representatives of their time. Write a paper elucidating the place of one of the following in this regard:

    John C. Calhoun   John Cotton
    Wendell Phillips   Eugene V. Debs
    Abraham Lincoln   Franklin D. Roosevelt
3. Journal articles often have useful historical material which

serves as background to the speakers. Select a recent article from the *Quarterly Journal of Speech, Speech Monographs, Southern Speech Journal,* or *Western Speech* and write a short paper appraising the handling of the historical materials.

4. Write an essay contrasting and comparing the use made of historical background in Vernon L. Parrington's *Main Currents in American Thought* with that of either Richard Hofstadter's *The Age of Reform,* or Ernest J. Wrage's and Barnet Baskerville's *American Forum.*

NOTES

1. Bower Aly and Grafton P. Tanquary, "The Early National Period: 1788-1860," in *History and Criticism of American Public Address,* William N. Brigance, ed. (New York: McGraw-Hill, 1943), Vol. I, pp. 64–65.
2. *Ibid.,* p. 65.
3. Ernest J. Wrage and Barnet Baskerville, *Contemporary Forum* (New York: Harper & Row, 1962), pp. 87–88.
4. Richard Hofstadter, *Great Issues in American History* (New York: Vintage Books, 1958), Vol. I, pp. 249–250.
5. Vernon L. Parrington, *Main Currents in American Thought* (New York: Harcourt, Brace, 1930), Vol. I, pp. 131–132.
6. *Ibid.,* pp. 162–163.
7. *Ibid.,* p. 178.

SELECTED BIBLIOGRAPHY

Brigance, William N., ed., *History and Criticism of American Public Address,* New York: McGraw-Hill, 1943, Vol. I, Chapters 1, 2, 3.

Hance, Kenneth G., "The Historical-Critical Type of Research: A Re-Examination," *The Central States Speech Journal,* XIII, 3 (Spring, 1962), 165–170.

Hofstadter, Richard, *Great Issues in American History,* New York: Vintage Books, 1958, Vols. I and II.

Parrington, Vernon L., *Main Currents in American Thought,*

New York: Harcourt, Brace, 1930, Vol. I, Part I, Chapters 1, 2.

Thonssen, Lester and A. Craig Baird, *Speech Criticism*, New York: Ronald Press, 1948, Chapter 10.

Wrage, Ernest J. and Barnet Baskerville, *American Forum*, New York: Harper & Row, 1960.

————, *Contemporary Forum*, New York: Harper & Row, 1962.

2 Historical Description and Analysis of Audience and Occasion

The study of historical materials in the preceding chapter has indicated that speeches are products of their time. One of the important issues in the presidential campaign of 1960, for example, was the so-called "space lag." Only a decade earlier, this problem could not have existed and a speaker would have looked foolish indeed had he made the "space lag" an issue in a political campaign. So, too, inversely, with the present. The problems of the "free coinage of silver" of William Jennings Bryan, of the "forgotten man" of Franklin D. Roosevelt, or of the "corrupt bargain" of Andrew Jackson obviously are not fitting as significant issues in a speech today.

The times, therefore, do mold the speakers' ideas, but so do the audiences and the occasions. One of the first duties of the public address critic, if he is to comprehend the efficacy of a speaker, analyze his rhetoric, or judge and assess the speaker's prowess, is to evaluate the nature of a specific audience at a critical juncture in history.

There are three simple categories of audience reaction. The first reaction is favorable to the speaker, his intentions and ideas. The second is one which is, or seems to be, completely opposed to the orator. The third is uncommitted, which seemingly neither favors nor opposes the speaker. Very seldom, however, can the critic find a pure reaction in any one audience.

One would think that if an audience were composed of political proponents, either of Republicans or Democrats, for example, it would be a favorable kind of audi-

ence. On certain issues this categorization may be close
to correct. There would be very few listeners in a purely
partisan audience of Republicans listening to former
President Eisenhower, to take an instance, who were
either uncommitted or opposed to the man and his views.
There may have been various degrees of enthusiastic
response, but probably little, if any, outright opposition.
On the other hand, even the delegates to the 1964 Republican Convention who listened to Senator Barry Goldwater give his acceptance speech hardly formed a pure
partisan audience. While there were very many delegates,
probably, who were committed to Goldwater by this time,
there were still a number who were opposed to the new
standard bearer and his views.

The audience which is completely hostile to a speaker
and his ideas is much more difficult to find. For obvious
reasons, speakers avoid such an audience. Nonetheless,
such audiences can be found. Colleges and universities
on occasion invite speakers such as avowed Communists,
for example, with whom the audiences almost completely
disagree. But even here, one can find among some students at least in sympathy with some of the ideals of
Marx. By their presence they therefore leaven the dough
of opposition, so that the speaker feels some favorable
rapport with the group. The audience, thus, is not completely hostile.

The neutral or uncommitted audience also is seldom
found in the "pure" sense. Probably no matter who the
speaker is, he may find some sympathetic faces and reactions to him and his proposals. The converse, of course,
is also true. Whether the audience has come to hear a
speech on outlawing the atomic bomb by Dr. Harold
Urey, on the expansion of civil rights by Senator Robert
Kennedy, on the broadening of educational opportunity
by President Lyndon B. Johnson, or on the advantages
of neo-orthodoxy in religion by Dr. Reinhold Niebuhr,
the very nature of these topics will almost immediately
force the listeners to take sides.

The simplistic breakdown of audiences into three major
categories, if only carried this far, is made only for the

most general purposes of analysis. But this can be a starting point for the critic of public address. From here he can begin to scrutinize the audience for trends and tendencies and emphases. Once he has ascertained what the dominant key to the audience is, then he can go about the task of determining how well the speaker adjusted to it, if at all. As a prelude to assessment, the public address critic's role here is not only to suggest that the adjustment was effective, mediocre, or a failure. This is patently not enough. His duty is to discover, if he can, how this adaptation by the speaker helped him to lead his audience, if not completely to his way of thinking, to his own view of "truth," then at least to a modification of the audience's own conceptions and views of "truth."

The audience, however, while an important facet of the total speaking situation, is only one such facet. The occasion is another. And to unearth the nature of the occasion is also a task of the critic. Often this is not as difficult as attempting to analyze the audience. Historical documents can usually be easily found indicating the reason for the meeting.

It can be a ceremonial occasion such as a dedication of a bridge, a dam, or a public building. Most often the speech is delivered by a noted political figure: a senator, a governor, a president. For example, Franklin Delano Roosevelt's speech, "Quarantine of Aggressor Nations Address" was made at the ceremonies dedicating Chicago's Outer Drive Bridge. It can be a group gathered because of some striking incident; as for example, the audience which met to hear Wendell Phillips, the great American orator, give one of his early, but monumental speeches, "The Murder of Lovejoy." It can be a regular meeting of a parliamentary, decision-making group, gathered to conduct the affairs within its charge. The meeting of the Senate to hear Daniel Webster give his great speech, "The Reply to Hayne," falls into this category. Or it can be a regularly scheduled meeting of a series of community forums dealing with topical problems of the day. Such a group might gather, for instance, to hear Dr. Reinhold Niebuhr discuss the relationship of religion and politics.

Whatever the occasion it is significant in rhetorical analysis and evaluation. It will, or at least it should, open another avenue down which the critic of public address may journey in his never-ending quest for rhetorical elucidation and assessment.

The aim of this search is to discover the factual and functional relationships among the speaker, the audience and the occasion. This is another important use of extrinsic factors in criticism. The first point, the search for an understanding of the times, focused on historical materials used as extrinsic factors of evaluation. The second one, the exploration of the composition of the audience and the reason for the occasion, brings the critic face to face with psychological and sociological factors for the same reason. These factors, as rhetorical scholars know, play a strong part in persuasion. Without a thorough comprehension and analysis of the psychological and sociological factors inherent in every audience and specific occasion, the critic, insofar as effective evaluation is concerned, would be lost indeed.

Moreover, the use of these extrinsic components, with their psychological and sociological overtones, is still only prelude. It is a prelude to the discovery and understanding of what the speaker actually did, from the standpoint of content and form, in adapting his message to the hearers within their immediate environment. Thus, the critic's analysis must also focus on the physical setting, as well as on the psychological and sociological ones already mentioned.

The physical environment of contemporary speechmaking does not pose the same problems as those of the past. This is due largely to mechanical devices such as public address systems and better acoustics. But the present brings on other, perhaps even more complicated difficulties. Moreover, the critic of public address needs to determine how a particular situation was handled by the speaker.

The problems, from the standpoint of adaptation and resolution, that faced Alexander Hamilton, for instance, were different when he spoke to a small group, such as President George Washington's cabinet, from when he addressed a much larger and diverse audience meeting in convention on the Federal Constitution. It is not merely the difficulty of coping with a different audience that was present on each occasion, but also of dealing with the contingencies of a different physical setting. Certainly the delivery had to be somewhat different in an intimate cabinet meeting as compared with the more open and formal convention audience. In what way did Hamilton cope with the varying exigencies of each situation? Can this be discovered by inference from the evidence of the speeches themselves? Must the critic look to other materials such as diaries, journals, memoirs, biographies, autobiographies, or histories? The questions, naturally, suggest the answers. All sources, whenever possible, need to be exploited in order to enhance comprehension and analysis. The secondary materials should be utilized for the extrinsic components, and the speeches themselves, as will be seen later on, for the intrinsic ones.

Modern times add further difficulties to those faced by Hamilton and his peers. Contemporary physical settings, as part of the speech occasion, may be similar in some ways, but they are also different. The contemporary speaker who is addressing a large audience may find that the physical setting plagues him with a two-pronged difficulty. Not only is he addressing the audience in the hall but often a larger one outside, through the modern media of radio and television. How did a speaker such as John F. Kennedy deal with this matter? The physical setting may have forced him to change his first inclination to speak extemporaneously from copious notes—as he often did on the campaign trail in 1960—to one which would tie him to manuscript, or in some cases to a teleprompter. Would this have made any difference in his presentation? And how would this have affected his style? Would he have to modify it? And what of the effect of this kind of physical setting on organization and invention? It is up to the critic of public address to come to grips with these difficulties. He does this by examining whatever sources are available, comparing and contrasting materials, weighing and evaluating them. Only then can the effect of the physical setting on the speaker be evaluated.

There are also psychological characteristics that affect the speaker as a result of the physical setting. Would a speaker for the John Birch Society be influenced in some manner if he were asked to speak in an AFL-CIO union hall? What would be the effect? Conversely, would the physical accoutrements of the Commonwealth Club of San Francisco sway in some way the speaking of a labor union representative? There is little doubt that all these would weigh psychologically in some fashion. But exactly how this would modify presentation and ideas would be the responsibility of the critic to unearth and assess.

Probably no one knew better than Henry Ward Beecher the psychological influence of physical setting upon himself as well as upon the audience. When his new church was being built, Beecher was very specific about the physical arrangements. He liked to have the audience all around him, not only in front of him. He felt that this wielded the most potent psychological impact, both upon himself and his audience. He had the feeling that he was most effective speaking under these physical conditions. And, his own confidence in the setting and his reaction to it influenced his relationship to his auditors. All this made for more effective persuasion.

Sociological factors also, especially those dealing with value systems, ideals, and prejudices, may in some way be a favorable or unfavorable influence on the speaker. These factors may be part of the setting. Placards containing slogans such as *"Liberté, Egalité, Fraternité,"* the "Right to Work," "Workers of the World Unite," the "Grand Old Party," and "The Lord Is My Shepherd" hanging on the walls of the meeting place probably work their subtle persuasion upon the speaker. Does the speaker make effective use of these slogans? Does he ignore them? Exactly how does he concern himself with them? Answers to these or similar questions will give useful discernment not only to the particular speaker-occasion-audience relationship, but to the character of the speaker as well. Thus, the situation can comprise one additional bit of evidence which the critic can use in constructing the total fabric of his evaluation.

Just as the physical setting may influence the speaker, so too do the ideas and philosophies of the audience itself. Here occasion and audience coalesce. This is particularly true when the function is a result of a public holiday, such as the Fourth of July or Memorial Day; or of the birthdays of well-known presidents, Washington, Jefferson, Jackson, or Lincoln; or of the celebrations commemorating the births or deaths of other notable figures in education, religion, or the arts, Horace Mann, Mary Baker Eddy, or Stephen Foster.

Audiences which come to such functions know that they will hear speeches extolling the ideas, concepts and social values of the individual being honored. There will be a great deal of talk relating these individuals and their accomplishments to a democratic society. In certain instances, the philosophies of the auditors are self-evident. The general values held by an audience at a Jefferson-Jackson Day Dinner is an instance in point. It can generally be assumed that the values of this group are somewhat different ideologically from those of persons attending a Lincoln Day Dinner. The first group is a Democratic aggregation, and the second is a Republican one. The first one, too, is probably more liberal in its conception of American society; the second one, more conservative. The former probably would extol the egalitarian virtues present in the Declaration of Independence, the Constitution of the United States, and in the mores of the society; the latter probably would emphasize the libertarian views within the above contexts. This again indicates that a description and analysis of the times are also needed, and must be coupled to a description and analysis of occasion and audience. It is not enough to *assume* that the views of the audience, as a result of the occasion, are the same at all times. External and internal evidence needs to be brought out to show similarities and differences. Certainly, at least, this much needs to be done if valid and reliable conclusions about the audience and occasion are to be made even in fairly self-evident rhetorical situations. But the difficulties of analysis in such homogeneous aggregations are not large.

The problem, on other occasions, however, can be more complex. The attempt to examine a heterogeneous audience from the standpoint of ideas and social values poses more difficulties. For instance, an audience at a World Affairs Council convention may hear different types of experts: military, civilian, political, social, educational, perhaps even religious. While there may not always be exactly the same audience (some members may not attend every session), there probably will be great similarities. But can one assume that the audience is also largely homogeneous in its concepts and philosophies? Probably not. About all one can infer from this niggardly data is that the group as a whole is interested in world affairs. But what its predilections are, insofar as military, political, civilian, social, educational, or religious affairs are concerned, is a moot point. Thus, the public address critic will find it difficult to determine the social values of such an audience. Nevertheless, since these external conditions make a great deal of difference in assessing the efficacy of a speaker, some attempt must be made.

A great difficulty in this kind of scholarly quest would be the paucity of materials available to the critic. Probably less material will be available about the audience than about the occasion, for obvious reasons. The lack of specific evidence means that conclusions are reached about audience and occasion based on some rather nebulous materials rather than on a solid foundation. This means further that in this area the critic is more fallible; he is open to adverse criticism if not outright condemnation.

Therefore, the critic should recognize his rather tenuous position and point out that his inferences are based on assumptions. The critic always needs to recognize, of course, that the discovery of more explicit materials about occasion or audience may modify his own assessment of the speaker. He should not feel irrevocably committed to a position at any time. If he did, the consequences for rhetorical scholarship would be disastrous. Patience, tentativeness, the willingness to change one's mind, these are the hallmarks of the critic; these are the prerequisites for growth and development.

Some rhetorical scholars have been able to describe and

analyze the occasions and audiences of specific speakers, even though they may not always have taken the additional step of evaluating the relationship of the speaker to occasion and audience. The essays in William N. Brigance's *History and Criticism of American Public Address* leave much to be desired in this regard. An examination of the studies show very few dealing specifically with occasion and audience. One notable exception is Forest L. Whan's study of Stephen A. Douglas, where he indicates the kinds of audiences that the Senator from Illinois faced. Of necessity somewhat general, since Whan's essay attempts to cover Douglas' total campaign for the senatorship in 1858, it nevertheless demonstrates the kind of scrutiny of occasion and audience that needs to be made. About the occasion, Whan says:

Speaking generally, the occasion for the campaign speeches made by Douglas in 1858 is so well known that it demands little explanation here. Douglas, a member of the Senate of the United States for nearly twelve years, was seeking re-election. Lincoln, a local politician and lawyer, who ten years earlier had served one term in the United States House of Representatives and who had left that body to find himself in disrepute at home, was opposing as the "unanimous choice" of the newly created Republican party. These men were not canvassing for votes for themselves but were working for votes for their colleagues, who were running for seats in the Illinois legislature. The legislature, in turn, would elect the Senator; the procedure followed in 1858. The issue was basically that of "popular sovereignty" for the newly created territories on the issue of slavery, versus the determined stand of the Republicans —"No more slave territory."

But beneath the surface of these well-known facts were many and varied matters that made the occasion of each speech a new and varied problem. If the occasion in general and the specific occasions discovered in different sections in particular are to be truly appreciated and evaluated, much more must be explained.

First of all, the battle was not a simple battle of campaign speeches between Douglas and Lincoln. Much of the actual work of the campaign was of necessity carried on by the newspapers. Further, each man could count upon the support of local men who were candidates in each district, and upon powerful allies brought in from outside the State. . . . They could depend upon allies in unvisited sections and could depend a great deal upon party ballyhoo.

A second factor, which added to the concern of Douglas and the joy of Lincoln, was the split within the Democratic party. Douglas' anti-Lecompton fight in the Senate, which he had just won against unbelievable odds, had embittered an already unfriendly administration toward him. Buchanan was determined to kill the Little Giant, even though it meant the election of a Republican Senator from Illinois.

A third factor that influenced a decision in preparing the campaign was that of the apportionment basis under which local legislators were elected and the location of what both parties knew to be "doubtful" districts. The 1850 apportionment basis was still in use, thus modifying a part of the tremendous increase in anti-slavery vote in the northern part of the state. . . .

A fourth factor in the campaign that Douglas recognized and attempted to meet was that of newspaper affiliation. . . . By 1856 most of the leading papers in northern Illinois were Republican. . . . But many new papers were established, most of them Democratic, supported financially by Douglas.

The fifth element of importance was that of the issues involved. Through its own organ each party stated the issue as it saw it. . . .

Thus, although the apparent issue between the two parties was that of popular sovereignty versus the demand of the Republicans for no more slave territory, the actual issue between Lincoln and Douglas was the ethical one of their relative consistency and honesty. Each was trying to build his own prestige in order to win the votes of the suspicious Germans and Whigs. Douglas fought the suspicion that he was in league with the South; Lincoln fought the suspicion that he was in league with the abolitionists.[1]

One can see from the above analysis that in delineating the occasion, Whan shows more than the mere physical or ceremonial aspects. He also concerns himself with the issues arising from the occasion and inextricably related to it, as well as the psychological and sociological factors underlying them. Whan's concern with the audience is well analyzed and articulated. He says:

The audiences that Douglas faced in the campaign of 1858 were a product of many trends that influenced the people of Illinois during the preceding decade. In order to understand fully what was in the minds of the people during the summer and fall of 1858, it is necessary to understand these trends.

The first influencing trend was that of a shift in population toward the West. The year 1848 marked the beginning of a new epoch in Illinois history. Before that date the state was filled largely with frontiersmen, most of whom came from the South; by 1858 these early settlers had moved on to California, Kansas, and Nebraska, leaving Illinois to the great influx of settlers from the East and abroad, who quadrupled the population of the state in ten years.[2]

A second trend of the fifties that affected the beliefs, attitudes and emotional character of the people in 1858 was the great development in agriculture and industry. The number engaged in agricultural pursuits doubled, acreage increased 73.7 per cent, and the value of farm property quadrupled.[3]

Industrially the state lagged behind agriculture, but manufacturing in this period advanced about 30 per cent. The value of raw materials was still not recognized by the populace. But the trend toward centralization of industry had already begun about Chicago. And although the panic of 1857 affected the farming portion of the state during the campaign year, Chicago remained relatively free from its influence.[4]

The economic beliefs of the people of Illinois that resulted from the trends just mentioned seemed to be as follows.[5] The horror of extravagance, the new attitude toward the tariff, the belief in the dignity of labor, and the experience with unemployment during the panic all had a vital influence on the 1858 campaign issues. Attitudes toward taxation, banking, and corporate enterprise, the acceptance of high rents and usury, and the lack of feeling of moral and social responsibility toward labor typifies stereotypes that affected acceptance of various arguments in the campaign.[6]

A third major trend, which must be understood to appreciate the beliefs and attitudes of the people of 1858, is that of increasing interest in and development of free educational opportunities. . . . By 1858 the superintendent was instrumental in building 3,000 schoolhouses, organizing

2,000 school districts, enrolling 440,000 students, or 14 out of every 15 children of school age, for an average term of 7 months. Free public high schools were established in the larger towns and cities, and no less than two dozen institutions of higher learning were incorporated. Although the fight for a state university failed and President Buchanan vetoed the land-grant bill of 1859, the struggle for free schools was indicative of the growing belief in democracy and equal opportunity for all, which was so important to Lincoln in the 1858 campaign.[7]

Thus we see that belief in educational and cultural development was crystallizing throughout the fifties and resulted in a school system, libraries, and various types of societies for intellectual development. The people were intellectually alert, extremely interested in politics, emotional in nature, and desirous of better education for their children. These things symbolized their sincere belief in the manifest destiny of the state, the Union, and democracy, and represented a growing tendency in Illinois to accept Republican philosophy.

Another institution experiencing great development during the decade was that of religion. The number of churches doubled during the decade; the value of church property quadrupled. To such an extent was church attendance considered necessary to good character that both Lincoln and Douglas were attacked in some quarters for their negligence in that matter. . . . Religious fervor typified the emotional character of the people, an element that strongly influenced Douglas and Lincoln in building their speeches for the 1858 campaign.[8]

Closely allied . . . was . . . Abolitionism, the radical anti-slavery movement. Until late in the decade, abolitionists were looked upon with displeasure, to say the least. It was not until the repeal of the Missouri Compromise, the publication of Mrs. Stowe's *Uncle Tom's Cabin,* the attempt at a more stringent Fugitive Slave Law, the Kansas-Lecompton Constitution fight, the Dred Scott decision, and the triumph of the Republican party in 1860 had each in turn influenced Northern and Western thought against slavery that Abolitionism ceased to be a curse to the hopeful politician, either Democratic or Republican, in Illinois.[9]

Thus the decade was marked by strong emotional trends in Illinois. And if one is truly to appreciate the emotional feeling of the time, the emotional character of the people

whom Douglas faced, he must remember that these movements were not mere passive undercurrents. They were
the moving spirit of political and social life. They swept
the state! Men did not merely believe or disbelieve in
these things, as do men of today. They felt keenly! They
fought mortal duels over these abstractions—even in the
United States Congress. The strength of their beliefs was
evidenced by their willingness to travel a hundred miles by
ox cart in wet weather to hear a single debate on one
of these subjects—days of hard, primitive travel. It was
further evidenced by men's willingness to give up friends,
money, business, or chance at personal gain in order to
settle Kansas to make it free or slave. It was evidenced
in growth of political parties on moral and emotional
issues alone. It was an emotional decade![10]

For obvious reasons, I have only used the more general
statements of Whan to give the reader a taste of the kind
of analysis in depth that is necessary for effective rhetorical assessment. I have not even touched upon the political
trends which are also part of the work. Whan's study
develops, in great detail, these and other factors affecting
the audience. But even the generalizations used here should
indicate the care with which Whan showed the reciprocity
that exists between audience and issues and their relation
to the speaker.

While the suggestions about the usefulness of the
occasion and audience have been treated in this chapter
as preludes to an understanding and assessment of a
particular speaker, the research and analysis going into
such a study may be of use in itself. In fact, if the assumption is true that anything shedding light on speaking,
be it description, analysis, interpretation, or criticism, has
intrinsic value, then studies, essays, or monographs dealing with audiences and occasions can shed further light
on public address and its criticism. This is not to say that
too much time has been spent on speakers in the past. It is
to say, rather, that not enough time has been spent on
audience and occasion. Such examinations make useful
materials for rhetorical assessment, both as part of a total
study, or for their own intrinsic merit.

QUESTIONS AND PROJECTS

1. What are the implications of Donald C. Bryant's reference to rhetoric—that is, to public address—as the art of adjusting ideas to people and people to ideas? Write a short essay showing the relationship and implications of the one to the other.

2. How valuable are the short introductions dealing with audience or occasion in A. Craig Baird's *American Public Addresses: 1740–1952*? Study especially the introduction to Henry Grady's speech on "The New South." Does it help you understand and evaluate Henry Grady's speaking prowess? In what way? Discuss these factors in a short analytical essay.

3. Examine the information on the audience and the occasion in Walter Emery's essay on "Samuel Gompers" in Volume II of the *History and Criticism of American Public Address* edited by William N. Brigance, and write a short paper analyzing its value.

4. Examine the material on the audiences faced by Harry Emerson Fosdick in the Robert D. Clark study in Volume III of the *History and Criticism of American Public Address* edited by Marie Hochmuth. Write a short paper evaluating its usefulness for an understanding of Fosdick.

5. Write a short essay on the speaker as a leader. It may be helpful to comment that the speaker's role is not only to adjust to a specific audience, but as a result of that adjustment, to lead the audience.

6. What are the different means used by speakers and writers to persuade their audiences? Do writers take into cognizance their audiences in the same way that speakers do? If not, how do writers think of their audiences? Write a short paper on your findings.

NOTES

1. Forest L. Whan, "Stephen Douglas," in *History and Criticism of American Public Address*, William N. Brigance, ed. (New York: McGraw-Hill, 1943), Vol. II, pp. 792–795.

2. *Ibid.,* p. 779.
3. *Ibid.,* p. 781.
4. *Ibid.,* pp. 781–782.
5. *Ibid.,* p. 782.
6. *Ibid.,* p. 785.
7. *Ibid.,* pp. 785–786.
8. *Ibid.,* pp. 786–787.
9. *Ibid.,* p. 788.
10. *Ibid.,* p. 789.

SELECTED BIBLIOGRAPHY

Auer, J. Jeffery, *An Introduction to Research in Speech,* New York: Harper & Row, 1959, Chapter 5.

Baird, A. Craig, *American Public Addresses: 1740–1952,* New York: McGraw-Hill, 1956.

Brigance, William N., ed., *History and Criticism of American Public Address,* New York: McGraw-Hill, 1943, Vols. I and II.

Bryant, Donald C. and Karl Wallace, *Fundamentals of Public Speaking,* New York: Appleton-Century-Crofts, 1960, Chapter 19.

Hochmuth, Marie, ed., *History and Criticism of American Public Address,* New York: Russell & Russell, Publishers, 1955, Vol. III.

Thonssen, Lester and A. Craig Baird, *Speech Criticism,* New York: Ronald Press, 1948, Chapter 12.

Vorys, John M., "How a Member of Congress Measures the Response of his Constituents," *Quarterly Journal of Speech,* XXXII, 2 (April, 1946), 170–172.

Wichelns, Herbert A., "The Literary Criticism of Oratory," in *Studies in Rhetoric and Public Speaking in Honor of James A. Wichelns,* New York: Century, 1925.

3 Biographical
Description
and Analysis

Biographical description and analysis are categorized here as external components, that is, factors outside the actual speech or speeches themselves. But since a speech is given by a specific individual, the information on the biography of a speaker also contains internal factors. This chapter, however, will focus on the external conditions of biography in the making of a speaker.

Despite the omnipresence of ghost writers and speech writers, especially in political speechmaking, a speech can be considered the product of a specific individual. Moreover, even though a specific speech may contain very little of the speaker's own rhetoric, it at least can be assumed to contain the nub of his ideas. And speeches, no matter how they are composed, are given by individuals. Thus the words themselves, as they come to the audience, are influenced by factors important in the individual, especially in his presentation. These are inherently part of him; they come from his life. This is one of the general reasons why the biography of a speaker should be studied; it provides discernments into the individual's speechmaking.

There is another reason related to the above but perhaps even more important. As a prelude to rhetorical assessment, biography is a significant factor in the scrutiny of an individual's *ethos*.

A speech, as every rhetorician since Cicero and Quintilian knows, can often be effective or ineffective as a result of the impact of the speaker's total personality. In fact, a strong case can be made for the Quintilian position of *ethos* as exemplifying the essence of an orator's potency. Barry Goldwater, it has often been said, even by his enemies, prospered in the political and speaking woods as a result of a very attractive personality. His personal appeal was such that it overrode many weaknesses in his logical argument. And Dwight Eisenhower, too, has scaled the heights of governmental service, not so much because of his ideas or arguments, but because of the power of his character. To discover how these mainsprings in a speaker's character, intelligence, and good will relate to his oratory is the aim of biographical description and analysis.

If the speech is primarily effective as a result of the speaker's total personality, some time should be given to the study of a speaker as a person. Probably the components which relate most explicitly to his speaking come from certain biographical data. Important facts are the speaker's place of birth and upbringing, his family background, his education, his training as a speaker, the nature of his early struggles, and any other experiences which may have molded his character.

The public address critic, if he is to understand and evaluate the object of his study, must go about this process in three ways. First, he must amass a great deal of pertinent material about his subject. Then, he must sift this for significant and salient details. Finally, he will need to analyze and even interpret the descriptive factual information to discover its relevance to the subject's speechmaking.

Where the person was born and raised can subtly influence his character and personality as well as his philosophy. It is easy to see that the orator's regional background will influence and affect his development in diverse ways. Would John C. Calhoun be the Calhoun we know, the cold, calculating, logical defender of the old South, no matter where he was born and brought up? Would Henry Clay be the Clay we know, the elegant, eloquent Great Pacificator, no matter where his early development took place? Would Daniel Webster be the Webster we are acquainted with, the powerful politico of Constitution and Union fame, no matter where he was raised? For example, what if Calhoun were born and received his early upbringing in New York rather than in South Carolina; Clay in New England rather than what was then the western frontier; and Webster in the deep southern delta rather than in New England? Would they have been the same great orators we now know? Probably not. The conditioning of time and place determined to some degree the development not only of each of these great orators' ideas, but even more importantly, those nebulous factors called character and personality.

So, too, with the orator's family background. Such eminent figures in public address as Wendell Phillips and Franklin D. Roosevelt probably would have been different, insofar as personality and character are concerned, if their family economic backgrounds, for example, were poverty-ridden rather than full of wealth. And who knows what the total *ethos* of Abraham Lincoln would have been had he been born in luxury rather than in a log cabin. He might not have been a politician at all. This is not to say, necessarily, that the individuals mentioned as examples would not have been interested in speechmaking, or not have succeeded at it. It is to say, and emphasize, that familial background and influence, not only economic, but social and intellectual as well, are important in understanding the power of the speaker's total personality.

Sometimes one can even discover specific character traits in one or the other of the subject's parents. The dourness or humor of a speaker, his friendliness or good will, his interest in the life of action or in the world of ideas, his religious cast of mind, his philosophical or metaphysical predilections, his idealistic or realistic approach to life's problems, and other characteristics of a similar nature can be traced to his immediate forebears. Such a discovery and delineation, which can border on the analytical and interpretative factors in biography, adds character interest to the study. In addition to that, however, the unearthing of such salient aspects of character can give helpful insights into the speaker's style and ideas as well.

As with his family background, so too with his educational one. It is easy to see, from the standpoint of speech analysis and evaluation, the importance of any training that the subject of the study might have had in actual speaking or debating in school. It is obvious, then, that the critic will try to unearth as much material of this type as he can, and relate it to the speaking of the individual. The critic's research into the educational background should not end here, however. After all, the speaker's main weapons are his thought, his ideas, and his predilections. Couple to that his style, language, arrangement, and presentation, and one can see the importance of describing and interpreting the speaker's education.

The fact that the orator was trained as a lawyer, a businessman, a minister, a priest, or a professor does make some difference in his outlook on life and in his speaking. There is little doubt, for instance, that the educational background and the intellectual interests of Woodrow Wilson were the keys to his oratorical success in some instances, and to his failure in others. According to some analyses of his speechmaking, the spiritual probings of his psyche in the League of Nations controversy also wielded an important influence. Finally, his own attitude toward his role in the quest for an enduring peace indubitably affected what he had to say and how he said it.

The importance of certain salient experiences which mold both the speaker's personality and his speaking is discernible. It has also been said of Woodrow Wilson that World War I with its wholesale slaughter of young men, especially of Americans, affected him greatly. The subsequent cynical machinations of European statesmen at the conference table also had their effect. Part of this effect, again according to some analytical interpretation, was a feeling of guilt. The feeling arose from the thought that he was the chief moving force in sending thousands of soldiers to their death in the war. This guilt, according to these scholars, he tried to expiate by organizing an international peace structure as a monument to the men who died, and to the wives, mothers, and fathers who suffered through their death. Not only were his ideas influenced by these experiences, but his *ethos* was affected as well. This, in reciprocal fashion, influenced his speaking. The public address critic not cognizant of these factors will go to his research and study with less than full discernment into the psyche of an orator such as Woodrow Wilson.

Thus the critic in describing the biographical details of a specific orator must constantly relate him as a person, as well as a speaker, to his time and his condition.

There will be many problems in the research and description of biographical details. Chief among these is the difficulty of finding materials of an objective nature upon which the critic of public address can build his own analysis and interpretations. Most biographers are anything but dispassionate. Most take a laudatory view of their subject. This is not unexpected, since the biographer spends a great deal of time with the subject of his study, and would hardly select a person completely antipathetic to his own views and nature.

The critic, to compensate for this omnipresent attitude in biographers, must look with a somewhat jaundiced eye upon the highly laudatory prose often written in biographies. This is especially true if the studies are early ones, that is, those written soon after the death of the notable figure. Winston Churchill's death, for instance, evoked many highly laudatory encomiums. These must be leavened with work of a more objective character. For this, comparisons with other sources are needed. Perhaps a useful method is to examine two other general areas of study as sources.

The first general area of scrutiny would be histories of the period. These may yield useful and pertinent information since historians, concerned with the large sweep of events and many individuals, are often more dispassionate. The second area would be works of a more primary nature. Memoirs, diaries, journals, even autobiographies if judiciously read can prove helpful. Eyewitness reports can also be of value. In this way, the critic of public address will have much diverse material on which to base his conclusions.

The method the critic will use to ascertain the truth and usefulness of materials is not unlike the one he utilized to validate historical materials of time and place discussed in the last chapter. The critic will use the same logical criteria as applied to authorities or expert testimony, since this is what the biographer really is. The critic must attempt to evaluate the reliability of the biographer's writings by looking for internal consistencies and inconsistencies. He will draw his conclusions to see if the biographer's statements generally conform to the accepted view of many scholars. If they do not, he should determine the reasons for the discrepancy and evaluate it with his own criteria. And, of course, he will determine whether the biographer comes to his conclusions on an adequate amount of valid and reliable evidence. This is most important. Here the public address critic's grounding in logic and argumentation should stand him in good stead.

Thus far, however, all that the critic has accomplished, if he has followed the above admonitions, is to gather factual biographical details. Useful as this is for a comprehension of the speaker under study, it is not enough. Now he must look beyond the biographical data, in order to analyze two large categories of biographical details.

First, the critic must decide where the speaker gets his power. Does it emanate from his knowledge, his intelligence, the thrust of his ideas, the cogency of his thinking? Does it come from stylistic factors, habits of preparation? Or does it stem from other factors such as personal power and reputation?

Second, the critic, must see whether the secret of the speaker's effectiveness comes from other factors, other sources. These, perhaps, might be more vague. They may be psychological and emotional factors exhibited by the speaker's voice, his dramatic sense, his physical appearance, his delivery, or his personal fighting attitude. By these criteria, the critic might try to determine whether Richard Nixon's selection, first as a vice-presidential, and later as a presidential candidate was due to aspects of character such as his fighting style and his effective argumentation, or whether it was due to other factors. Some critics would say that his political defeat came from the lack of some of these characteristics in his debates with John F. Kennedy. The belief that Nixon had had these qualities at one time, but had lost them during the debates, might have strengthened the belief that he was on the downgrade as a debater and politico. These assumptions by the audiences Nixon addressed might very easily have weakened his persuasive ability.

Other rhetoricians and even historians would say that Harry S. Truman's victory over Thomas E. Dewey in the 1948 presidential election was due in large part to similar characteristics. Dewey, it may be recalled, was the predicted winner. His defeat by Truman, these analysts would say, was largely due to Truman's never-say-die attitude and his fighting speeches from the rear car of his special campaign train. There is some merit in this analysis.

The difficulties in determining the value of the analytical biographical details are similar to those encountered in deciding the usefulness of biographical description. The public address critic must look for the significant biographical data and ascertain the relevance of this material to his total analysis. Moreover, the inferences drawn from his analysis of the material must follow accepted rational lines. The critic needs to use his training in evidence and reasoning—in argument in a practical sense—so that his own analysis will have logical consistency, validity, and reliability.

The novice in public address analysis and criticism can be aided by looking at examples of biographical factual material and analysis. Robert T. Oliver shows the significance of character as an aid to understanding the speaker in his analysis of Thomas Hart Benton, "The Magnificent Missourian." Oliver states in his *History of Public Speaking in America:*

> Thomas Hart Benton was an orator in spite of his speeches—a living exemplar of the theory that oratory is more than the verbal text; it is, in the end, man speaking. His dynamic personality did much to shape the course of events during one of the most crucial generations of American history.
>
> Benton's life commenced in failure. He was born in 1782, and six years later his father died. In due course he entered the University of North Carolina, where he made a name as a debater in the literary societies but was expelled for stealing money from several fellow students.

Mrs. Benton then moved her family to Tennessee to escape the shadow of this disgrace, rearing her family in debt and hoping for eventual income from her late husband's large investment in unsettled lands. Benton became a successful lawyer and won election to the State Senate on the strength of his attacks against the cumbersome judicial system. Then came the War of 1812, and Benton strove valiantly to make a name for himself as a Colonel of Militia. Through misunderstandings generated by jealous rivals, he was represented to General Andrew Jackson as a glory seeking incompetent and was kept remote from battle. As a result, on September 4, 1813, when he and Jackson met unexpectedly in a Nashville hotel lobby, both men drew pistols and Jackson's left shoulder was shattered. Benton was thereafter continually beset by bullies who tried to force him into a duel to revenge the wounding of Tennessee's popular hero. In 1815 he fled to St. Louis, once more to start life anew after an irremedial failure.

Missouri was a goldmine of disputed land claims, following the expulsion of the French and Spaniards; Benton mastered both the French language and French law, with which knowledge he soon became a flourishing success. Then, in 1817, he made what he always thought to be the worst mistake of his life. As a result of a trifling exchange of words following a court case, he hounded Charles Lucas, the opposing attorney, until he forced him into a duel. In the first fight, at a distance of thirty feet, Lucas was wounded. Benton refused to let the matter drop, and engineered another encounter at ten feet. Lucas was killed. Benton was soon overcome by remorse, and during the remainder of his life managed to evade duels, though many efforts were made to force him to fight. Until the last ten years of his life, he even curbed his quick-blazing temper; when it finally burst from control, he paid for it with his career.[1]

Even such a capsule profile illustrates that biographical details are helpful in comprehending and analyzing the Benton personality.

It is not necessary to quote from that old master of biographical materials, Vernon L. Parrington. Speech critics can find a fund of materials in his *Main Currents in American Thought*. His analyses of the character and personality of John C. Calhoun, Ralph Waldo Emerson, and Theodore Parker are especially striking. The nascent critic of public address should note how effectively Parrington welds this biographical information in making judgments not only about the character, but also about the ideological predilections and literary and rhetorical accomplishments of the objects of his study.

Another interesting and useful example of this type of biographical research can be found in A. E. Whitehead's essay on that great American enigma, William E. Borah. This appears in Volume III of the *History and Criticism of American Public Address*. In a pithy analysis only three pages in length, Whitehead delineates the main factors which influenced Borah as politician and speaker. Whitehead states:

> Borah's early background offers some clue to the understanding of this baffling and contradictory man. . . .
>
> As a youth, he was impressed with the gentleness and kindness of his mother, traits that he displayed in personal relationships. His father was stern and austere; he expected and received obedience. Between him and his son, however, existed a bond of mutual respect and confidence. Although disciplined in an exacting manner, Borah admitted that there was justice and reasonableness in his father's demands upon his children.
>
> Possibly the most important influence exerted by Borah's father was religious. He was a leader in the Presbyterian church and a constant reader of the Bible. Borah did not accept his father's fundamentalist view, but he was impressed by his father's charity and tolerance, and they seemingly served as a basis for his philosophy in such matters as race prejudice, persecution of war prisoners, and religious intolerance. . . .
>
> Borah's concern for and his advocacy of those in the lower economic strata, his advocacy of free speech for minority groups, his advocacy of justice and tolerance for Soviet Russia and Mexico, and his advocacy of the plain people in the League of Nations and the World Court disputes may well be attributed to the moral teachings of his father. . . .
>
> An important factor in Borah's development as a speaker was his prolific reading begun as a youth and continued throughout life. While his law practice was expanding, he studied history, government, law. He read the speeches of Cicero, Demosthenes, Sheridan, Fox, Pitt, Burke, Lincoln,

Douglas and Phillips.

In addition to this reading, he still had time for novels and poetry. . . .

Borah believed that anyone taking part in American public affairs ought to make himself familiar with the writings of Hamilton, Jefferson, Madison, Washington, and others who determined the nature of the Constitution. These men he quoted with ease.

This independent and individualistic man who became the spokesman for political isolationism was born in Lincoln's state. The Borah family shared the common feeling of many who tended toward deifying both Lincoln and Washington. Washington's injunctions against interweaving our destiny with that of any part of Europe became Borah's thesis in his anti-League of Nations speech given in the Senate on February 21, 1919. . . .

Finally, Borah's early training in the frontier civilization of Idaho became an important factor in determining his political philosophy. Borah represented the independence of a pioneer region in which individualism was a dominant culture-pattern. His attitude toward world affairs was linked with the mental aloofness of a state which nurtured his independence. The essence of Borah was self-sufficiency and independence, and he never went through the transition of a desire to conform.[2]

A recent essay appearing in *Western Speech* by Ernest J. Wrage couples succinct biographical details with cogent rhetorical and political analysis. Wrage gives lucid insights into Barry Goldwater as orator and statesman in the piece entitled, "The Little World of Barry Goldwater." While hardly as definitive in biographical description and analysis as the Whitehead study on Borah, Wrage does make some useful points in his short analytical critique. He says:

An Arizona storekeeper, Barry Goldwater was first elected to the Senate in 1952, a Republican in a nominally Democratic state. He's a man of considerable substance and small learning. He flunked out of public high school in his freshman year, graduated from a military academy with distinction in military subjects, and failed to complete his freshman year at the University of Arizona. Evidently though, the Senator is not at all embarrassed in making *ex cathedra* pronouncements on the content and methods of contemporary education, publicly deploring as he does the domination of schools by the progressivism of John Dewey and his disciples.

Goldwater's early political capital consisted of a family name prominent in Arizona, a war record, and a wide acquaintance with Genus Arizonus gained through chatty talks while showing colored slides on Indians of the Southwest. He came to national attention through tele-vised hearings on labor racketeering, his bitter-ender speech on the Kennedy-Ervin Labor Bill, and his opposition to the Rockefeller-Nixon "New York Munich pact" at the time of the 1960 Republican Convention. The big reception accorded him by the Convention turned him into circuit rider in behalf of his brand of political fundamentalism and won for him the sobriquet of Mr. Conservative.[3]

These two excerpts illustrate two highly different ap-proaches and styles in writing biographical details as aspects of rhetorical evaluation. Both, however, are grounded in probing and effective scholarly research. Whitehead's is tentative, objectively searching, while Wrage's is bolder and more personal. Each, however, has its place in public address criticism.

Another relationship that can help us understand and evaluate the speaker is the relationship of invention to *ethos*, of ideas to character. My own interest in this area of study has brought out the fact that while invention and *ethos* are not biographical details of the same nature as those previously discussed, they are also important, to rhetorical assessment. It illustrates, too, how difficult analysis—breaking down a totality into easily discernible and discreet segments—really is. Part of any biographical study is a comprehension of a man's political thought, especially if he is a politician. Alexander Hamilton, the great orator, is an intriguing subject for such an analysis. In studying the relationship of such a man's *ethos* to his ideas, it is necessary to look at the evaluations of his biographers and critics. Hamilton, according to some of these, has been misunderstood. Professor Bower Aly, emi-nent rhetorician, is an instance in point. He indicates in an essay on "Alexander Hamilton's Year" that probably "no other great American has been so consistently misrepresented and misunderstood as Alexander Hamilton. Even men who should know better have attacked Hamilton for saying, 'Your people, sir, is a great beast.' With equal indiscretion, those who admire Hamilton have sometimes endeavored to justify a statement that has never been authenticated."[4] And Louis M. Hacker, prominent historian, has on occasion given Hamilton more than customary homage for his contribution to the American Republic. In this way he sought to improve Hamilton's character.

There is little doubt, however, that the prevailing conclusions about Hamilton, to which Aly, Hacker, and others object, are fairly well founded. Moreover, even if Hamilton never did make the statement, "Your people, sir, is a great beast," his life and political thought indicate that the canard does sound like Hamilton after all. To see this distrust of the common man, one need only look at salient facets of his biography. Alexander Hamilton

> had only contempt for the weaknesses of the Constitution of the United States with its representative equality. Instead, he even defended the notorious corruption of the British Parliament, saying that it was expedient. . . .
>
> The precedent of British Parliament gave Hamilton another argument which again illustrates his innate distrust of the people. This is his theory of so-called "virtual representation." This idea was first articulated by Edmund Burke and utilized in England by those who were interested in maintaining the substance of aristocracy. This was accomplished through the device of couching the idea in democratic terms. It is *The Federalist* No. 35 that Hamilton argues for "merchants" to represent "mechanics," and for "land holders" to be the natural representatives of those who actually till the soil. All this, of course, also lends credence to the view that Hamilton regarded democratic representation as exceedingly weak.
>
> But the impracticability of a representative government was not the only aspect of the idea of democracy which was distasteful to Hamilton. His contempt for the populace is further illustrated in one of the articles in the Daily Advertiser, which he signed—and here is a suggestive indication of character and reputation—Caesar. "For my part," he declared, "I am not much attached to the *majesty*

of the multitude, and therefore waive all pretentions (founded on such conduct), to their countenance. I consider them in general as very ill qualified to judge for themselves what government will best suit their peculiar situations; nor is this to be wondered at. The science of government is not easily understood."

From the above, therefore, it can readily be inferred that only educated men like himself were competent enough to judge government. Equal status and responsibility were thus denied the common people.[5]

There is little doubt that the aspects of Hamilton's thought contained in the preceding excerpt had ramifications for his character.

Journals, biographies, critical studies and monographs are replete with material that is useful not only as a part of a full scale study of a speaker, but also in itself. While it is not the public address critic's prime responsibility to write biography, nothing should prevent the critic from doing independent work of this nature. Historians and literary critics are not alone in having the qualification for this kind of study. Rhetoricians and public address critics come as well equipped. As a matter of fact, this study, which can result in books, articles, and monographs, can add a significant page to the history of public address and to the history of American culture as well.

QUESTIONS AND PROJECTS

1. Write a short essay on ethical proof showing the similarities and differences between it and logical proof.
2. How does *ethos* manifest itself in a speech?
3. In what specific ways does ethical proof help the speaker?
4. Write a short paper relating the components of *ethos* to the five canons of oratory. Wherein is *ethos* most important? Wherein least?
5. Write a paper evaluating the qualities of character which helped to make Franklin D. Roosevelt an effective speaker.
6. In what way did Richard M. Nixon use proof by per-

sonality in the 1960 presidential campaign?
7. In what way did John F. Kennedy use proof by personality in the 1960 presidential campaign?
8. Examine the biographical details in Whitehead's "William E. Borah" carefully. Do a similar biographical sketch of a contemporary speaker, Senator Wayne Morse of Oregon, for example, or Senator Everett Dirksen of Illinois.
9. Write a short paper agreeing or disagreeing with the following statement: "The most important factor in the success of a speaker is his ethical appeal."

NOTES

1. Robert T. Oliver, *History of Public Speaking in America* (Boston: Allyn and Bacon, 1965), pp. 130–131.
2. A. E. Whitehead, "William E. Borah," in *History and Criticism of American Public Address*, Marie Hochmuth, ed. (New York: Russell & Russell, Publishers, 1955), Vol. III, pp. 366–369.
3. Ernest J. Wrage, "The Little World of Barry Goldwater," *Western Speech*, XXVII, 4 (Fall, 1963), 210.
4. Bower Aly, "Alexander Hamilton's Year," *Quarterly Journal of Speech*, XLIII, 4 (December, 1957), 427.
5. Anthony Hillbruner, "Invention and Ethos: The Metamorphosis of Alexander Hamilton," *Central States Speech Journal*, XI, 1 (Autumn, 1959), 44–45.

SELECTED BIBLIOGRAPHY

Hillbruner, Anthony, "Invention and Ethos: The Metamorphosis of Alexander Hamilton," *Central States Speech Journal*, XI, 1 (Autumn, 1959), 44–45.
———, "Word and Deed: Jefferson's Addresses to the Indians," *Speech Monographs*, XXX, 4 (November, 1963), 328–334.
Lee, Irving J., "Some Conceptions of Emotional Appeal in Rhetorical Theory," *Speech Monographs*, VI (1939), 66–86.

Quintilian, *Institutes of Oratory*, trans. by H. E. Butler, London: Loeb Classical Library, 1921, 1922, 4 vols.

Sattler, William M., "Conceptions of *Ethos* in Ancient Rhetoric," *Speech Monographs*, XIV (1947), 55–65.

Thonssen, Lester and A. Craig Baird, *Speech Criticism*, New York: Ronald Press, 1948.

Walter, Otis M., "Toward an Analysis of Ethos," *The Pennsylvania Speech Annual*, XXX (1964), 37–45.

Yeager, W. Hays, "Wendell Phillips," in *History and Criticism of American Public Address*, William N. Brigance, ed., New York: McGraw-Hill, 1943, Vol. I.

4 Historical Description and Analysis of the Effects of Speeches

The final extrinsic factor to be discussed before examining the speeches themselves is the significant component of the effect of speechmaking. This effect can be considered and analyzed in a single speech, a series of speeches, a debate, a series of debates, or perhaps even the larger scope of the total speechmaking of an individual orator.

The general aim of the critic of public address is to discover what happened as a result of a given speech or a series of speeches. Specifically, such a study can take two distinct routes. The first is to determine the immediate effects of the speech. The second is to discover what the long range effects were. The critic can emphasize the one or the other of these areas, or obviously, he can deal with both, showing relations, comparisons, contrasts.

The immediate effects of a speech are often not too difficult to ascertain. A case in point might be some effective Congressional or Senatorial oratory, such as Senator Robert A. Taft speaking against foreign aid. If, as a result of a speech or a series of speeches, Taft could have gotten his Senatorial peers to cut the allocations for foreign aid, obviously his speaking would have had an immediate effect. However, the critic needs to be tentative. He cannot say without reservation that it was the effectiveness of the Senator's speaking alone that brought about the desired result. After all, in political situations there are many factors leading to a particular conclusion. Nevertheless, the public address critic can scrutinize the political and rhetorical situation and ascertain to what degree a particular speech did bring about a certain desired result. He can even discern the unique factors in a speech that led to the desired end. Such a scrutiny, however, begins to move into the realm of analysis, about which more will be said later.

To point out an instance of the immediate effect of a single speech, one need only look at Richard M. Nixon's "Checkers" speech. During the 1952 presidential campaign, there was some question of the financing not only of Nixon's political campaigns, but of a so-called "slush" fund established for his private expenses as well. This fund was ostensibly maintained by wealthy private groups in California. The accusations grew so heated that both the Republican party and Dwight D. Eisenhower, the party's presidential nominee, wondered if Nixon would be more of a hindrance than an asset in the forthcoming campaign.

As a result of the hullabaloo created in newspapers and other communication media, Richard M. Nixon appeared on television. His avowed purpose was to absolve himself of the charges and thereby remain as Eisenhower's running mate. Nixon's speech was a creative amalgam of emotional, ethical, and logical appeals, with the first the dominant one. It proved so impressive that Nixon cleared himself of much of the onus that existed earlier. He re-established himself as a man of integrity and honor. It was so effective that Eisenhower, in a now famous statement, said that Nixon was as clean as a hound's tooth. The Republican party, with Eisenhower and Nixon as its standard bearers, claimed an overwhelming victory. This is a clear instance of the successful result of a single speech. Nixon's avowed purpose of exculpating himself and of staying on as a vice-presidential candidate was successfully achieved. The television speech, reaching millions, had attained its desired end.

Another effect of the Nixon speech, in addition to that of keeping him on the Republican ticket, was the enhancement of his own reputation. Until the speech, Nixon's character had been at a low ebb in the eyes of the public. While the speech did not completely vindicate him, it did add to his ethical stature in the opinion of many people, perhaps even the majority. Very few speeches have done more.

To find the immediate results of a speech, the critic needs to gather historical data of a descriptive nature. At times this information is readily available; at other times it is more obscure. The Nixon-Kennedy debates in the 1960 presidential election fall somewhere in between. That they are notable exemplars of immediate effects there is little doubt. But what the immediate effects were is perhaps not as clear. Certainly this is not as clear as in the Nixon television appearance in the "Checkers" speech. Many rhetoricians, historians, and journalists have agreed that Kennedy's impressiveness in the debates made the difference between defeat and victory in the election.

Many speeches have an even less obvious purpose and effect than the Nixon-Kennedy confrontations. It is true, for example, that Abraham Lincoln's "Gettysburg Address" had a significant purpose and an important result, but one more difficult to measure. As a eulogy in the tradition of Pericles' "Funeral Oration," it was more nebulous in construction, aim and results. Probably all one could say was that the "Gettysburg Address" was successful because it made men think. Even this effect, however, was not readily discernible if the address were to be measured by the applause that it received at its conclusion. While demonstrative applause is a shaky criterion of the ultimate success or failure of a particular address, it is an indicator of the immediate effect. Most speakers are aware of the value of this hallmark. Certainly Lincoln was. In fact, the dearth of demonstration, it has been said by historians, made Lincoln feel that the address was a failure. This ostensible failure was more evident when compared with the reception given Edward Everett's lengthy oration on the same occasion. The latter was greeted with an overwhelming ovation at its conclusion. The "Gettysburg Address" thus hardly seemed a roaring success in terms of its immediate results.

But what of the long range results of Lincoln's speech? Lincoln's address is a prime example of this second consideration in discovering the effectiveness of a speech. The critic of public address can assume, on the descriptive level, that the lastingness of a speech such as the "Gettsyburg Address" means that it has had its effects far beyond its immediate environs. It means that it impressed many more individuals than that group which listened to it on the battlefield near Gettysburg, Pennsylvania. The fact that school children still memorize the "Gettysburg Address" is sufficient evidence.

There is other evidence of its impressive long range results. Numerous analyses by literary and rhetorical critics point to its lastingness. Historians and political theorists unearth significant social and political concepts of a functioning democratic society in its paragraphs. Politicians and statesmen use its ringing words to support their ideas in times of crisis. It has had its impact on the civil rights movement of the 1960's. Parodies of it have been written to show the superiority of the original product. It is a short speech packed with ramifications, some of which are still unexplored and unexploited.

Not all speeches, however—even great ones—have such obvious lasting effects as Lincoln's memorable address. The research problem for the rhetorical critic in finding immediate and long range results is the usual one of unearthing significant historical material which will reveal the needed information. The public address critic soon becomes aware that to make effective and useful discernments into the immediate and long range results of a speech, he must spend a great deal of time in scholarly digging. The effort will be well worth the time and energy expended.

Useful as this is, it is not enough merely to describe the effect—immediate or long range—of a given speech or speaker. Actually, the role of the public address critic is much larger. Unfortunately, however, much scholarly writing of an ostensibly critical nature stops at this juncture. If critics are to make useful contributions to rhetoric and to society, they must do much more. One job is to analyze and interpret the results of the speaking. To this end he must ask himself such questions as the following:

Why did the orator succeed in his aim? Or, if he only partially succeeded, what were the reasons for the partial success? And, of course, if the speech failed completely, at least in immediate results, why did it fail?

Answering questions of this type can be a challenging invitation to the critic's abilities in research, insight and analysis. He must gather the data and draw inferences from it which have validity and reliability. To this end he must spend some time on the speech itself. How this is to be done will be discussed in the chapters dealing with the intrinsic factors of a speech. Before an actual scrutiny of the speech itself is made, the critic can check secondary sources: newspapers, magazines, periodicals, histories, and biographies. After the material has been gathered, he will again need to sift and weigh, to analyze and interpret, and finally to draw his own conclusions.

For example, just because a newspaper columnist has indicated that the failure of a specific speech was due to its poor delivery, does not necessarily mean that this was actually so. The public address critic should seriously consider this assessment. He should also study the rhetorical credentials of the writer. And he should compare the particular article with similar ones before accepting, rejecting, or modifying the columnist's conclusions. Of course, some columnists are a good deal better than others at analyzing and evaluating speeches. Richard H. Rovere, the writer and columnist, has discounted his abilities as a formal speech critic. His "Letter from Washington," which appears occasionally in *The New Yorker*, however, belies this self-effacing statement. Incisive and insightful, it often contains valuable analyses of important public addresses. His scrutiny of Senator Fulbright's foreign policy address in the spring of 1964 shows his understanding of some important aspects of rhetorical analysis.[1] His evaluation in *Harper's Magazine* of Barry Goldwater's thought and speech is notable for dissecting the logical inconsistencies of that conservative champion's argument.[2] The public address critic would do well to incorporate some of Rovere's discernments in his own analyses of contemporary political speakers. Since not every columnist is a Richard H. Rovere, however, the critic needs to be exceedingly careful in using such material in his own critical assessments.

The nascent critic should now be quite aware of the hazards in attempting to analyze and interpret the results of speechmaking. Analyses and interpretations of the effects are much more difficult than the mere description of what happened on the factual level as a result of a single speech, or a group of them. It is more difficult to evaluate the immediate and long range results. It is more difficult because these results are related to all the factors in the speaking of an individual. This cannot be over-emphasized.

More specifically, by utilizing some of the factors discussed in the chapter on audience and occasion, one could determine that the prime reason for the failure of an address was lack of comprehension by the audience. That the speaker's proposals were ahead of the thinking of the audience might be a factor. Or perhaps, to consider some of the historical components of time and place, the critic may discover that the socio-cultural construct of the times is not ready for the changes the speaker proposes; that in some manner the speaker is not only too far ahead of his audience, but ahead of the times in which the specific audience functions as well. Thus, his speaking may be more influential a decade, a generation, or a century later than it was during his own time.

Then, too, speakers may call upon the audience to resurrect long dead ideas and values. While there is often a nostalgia in many audiences for the rugged virtues of our forebears, this nostalgia is usually more theoretical than practical. Audiences today, affected by increased educational opportunities, the growth of the mass media, as well as the development of sophisticated attitudes towards their own times, are hardly naive. On the contrary, they are more often highly practical and realistic. So while speeches which call for a society in which each one is responsible for himself may evoke nostalgic reminiscences of our pioneer forefathers, that is generally all they do accomplish. The common man who comprises a major part of most audiences is not so common today.

He well realizes the gains and values of the modern comforts surrounding him. He is not to be seduced easily by calls to the vigorous life, calls made so magnificently by Teddy Roosevelt, and to which audiences of an earlier time and an earlier persuasion were so responsive. Therefore, while a speaker may exude a certain charm and power by holding such an attitude, as did Senator Barry Goldwater, he will often fail in his immediate ends because time has passed him by. The ultra-conservative who pleads for the abolition of the income tax, unemployment insurance, or social security soon discovers that while the audience would like some of the benefits that would result from a possible change, it intuitively feels that it would lose more than it would gain by a radical change in policy, economic or otherwise.

It may be, however, that certain alterations advocated by an orator, even though they seem regressions to a distant past, may find a quickening response in the audience. The winds of political and social doctrine blow hot and cold. It is up to the critic of public address to analyze their potency at the time of the speech, attempt an interpretation which may explain the apparent failure or success of the speaker.

But in speechmaking, the call for forward moving or backward looking alterations in society need not only be analyzed and interpreted in terms of that time, useful as such scrutinies may be. Public address plays a larger role in society. As a result of studying certain seminal speeches and lectures, one can discern the historical precedents for ideas currently in vogue. Consider Ralph Waldo Emerson as a thinker and lecturer. While there is little doubt that his great addresses, "The American Scholar," "The Divinity School Address," "Nature," and others were influential in directing the American mind toward a more optimistic view of society and religion, the full ramifications of his views were not immediately discernible. His own audiences and his own times did not immediately see the full impact of his words.

Even a cursory examination of the results of some of these addresses will show the public address critic that while "The American Scholar" was greeted with huzzas and accolades of every description, its religious counterpart, "The Divinity School Address," was not as successful. Why not? There are many reasons, and it is dangerous to oversimplify them. However, an important one that critics and scholars have discerned was that while the people in the audience were willing to accept the intellectual ramifications of the kind of transcendental freedom that Emerson preached, they were not as willing to adopt the religious ones. In other words, while they were eager to apply the individualistic injunctions to their intellectual and practical life, they were not as ready to apply them to their metaphysical and religious one.

The public address critic, looking at the addresses within the context of the times, the audience, and the occasion, could rightfully say that "The American Scholar" attained its immediate objective, while "The Divinity School Address" did not. Moreover, the critic probably would be right.

Do past public addresses also have important consequences for the present? If so, in weighing the effect of a particular address upon subsequent generations, the critic will need to make a different analysis and interpretation. The voice of Emerson, in such an examination, will be seen to ring across the channel of time with influences on the future not even dreamed of at the time the original speech was given. Thus, the consequences of an influential address on later American civilization can be as important, if not more so, as on the contemporary society.

Another example of a great speech which wielded significant influence on the future is Daniel Webster's "Reply to Hayne." Delivered in the United States Senate on January 26 and 27, 1830, it has been loudly and justly praised for its distinct and immediate accomplishments. From the point of view of this discussion, however, it achieved two prime results. First, at a time when American orators and statesmen were having the great dialogue concerning state or federal pre-eminence in the development of the country, Webster's speech threw its weight with the people and federalism, and against the states and state sovereignty. Webster accomplished this by the rigor of his arguments, and by his theoretical and philosophical grounding in the concepts of the particular audience of senators. Consequently, he gained important immediate results, one of which was the granting of jurisdiction over the western lands—not to the states, but to the federal government.

The second result was the acceptance, as precedent and law, that the power of the United States issued from the people (the Northern argument), rather than from the states (the Southern argument). To be concise, this meant that the Constitution was now interpreted as a contract entered into by all the people of one nation, rather than by the states themselves. The results of the adoption of this doctrine so impressively brought out in Webster's address are obvious. American society today is greatly, if not completely, dependent upon it. In the world community, we probably could not function without it. This effect of the speech upon the present, and perhaps upon the future, is as important as its result was in Webster's day.

Many speeches of this type have become public documents, almost as strong as precedents, acts, laws, and Supreme Court decisions. They have been quoted by subsequent generations of orators, politicians, and statesmen. The influence of George Washington's "Farewell Address" has been tremendous since it was given almost a century and three-quarters ago. Certainly its effect was not confined to his own time. In all probability the road taken by the United States in foreign affairs would have been quite different if Washington's address had presented another viewpoint or even had it not been given. So, too, with other salient orations, such as Thomas Jefferson's "First Inaugural Address," Booker T. Washington's "Atlanta Exposition Address," and Abraham Lincoln's "Second Inaugural Address." To further illustrate this residual power, one need only look at the reception Lincoln's address received. The *London Spectator* lauded the speech as "the noblest political document known in history, and should have for the nation and the statesmen he left behind him, some of sacred and almost prophetic authority."[3]

These few examples should point out to the public address critic that there are difficult problems in the analysis and interpretation of the effects of speechmaking. While it is true that most examination of the results of speechmaking tend to focus on immediate effects, and probably should do so, the critic should not ignore the long range results of particular speeches. It is almost virgin soil, which can be exploited by scholars and critics interested in discovering and evaluating the on-going influence and role of public address in the American democratic society.

This is not to say that critics have not done yeoman labor in both fields of immediate effects and long range results. The essay on "Dwight L. Moody" by Robert Huber in the third volume of the *History and Criticism of American Public Address* to some degree assays both roles. Moody was the famous evangelist who conducted a number of revivals in America and Britain. After analyzing Moody as a speech personality, the speeches which stirred the crowds, the psychological factors peculiar to his audiences, and the cultural context, Huber asks, "What were the results, the reactions to the revivals?" In a long conclusion to his study, Huber analyzes the immediate effects as follows:

The number of people attracted to attend the revival meetings furnishes our first clue. So great was the attendance that the meetings attracted the attention of the newspapers and religious magazines of the day. Their estimates furnish the evidence of Moody's power to draw crowds to hear him preach. The attendance at the series of revivals in Great Britain and America from 1873 to 1877 was the largest. The average attendance at the first meetings, held in York, was small; the largest single audience numbered only about one thousand. But they grew larger as time elapsed and as he visited larger cities. The peak attendance at Sunderland was 3,000; at Glasgow, the evening service often drew 10,000, and overflow meetings were held for those unable to gain admittance. Dublin, Manchester, and Liverpool produced even larger crowds. More meetings were held each day. London was the climax of the British tour. The first series of meetings was held in the northern part in Agricultural Hall, which was equipped to seat 13,700. Frequently it was full, and the average daily attendance for the first few weeks was 20,000. On Sunday, April 4, 1875, Moody spoke to 40,000 persons. After the London series was over the committee in charge reported . . . [that] during the four months in London, Moody's revivals attracted 2,500,000 persons.

The size of the audience attending the Moody revival meetings in the United States equaled those in Great Britain. . . .

Our second clue to the results of the revivals of the evangelist should be found in the number of converts. With Moody, however, the only evidence for the number of converts may be found in the reports of the early years. He was very careful to avoid publication of these results. In fact, he insisted that whether a man was converted or not was between the man and his God. He sought constantly to check those who might try to count the number of converts. There were clues, however, in the attendance at meetings for converts only, where admission was by ticket. There were 400 converts at Sunderland, 3,500 present at the last converts' meeting in Glasgow, and 3,000 at a similar meeting in Dublin. The ministers of London estimated that 7,000 had been converted during the four months of revival services there. The last meeting for converts in New York was attended by 4,000, and the same number attended a similar meeting in Chicago.[4]

The third clue to the results or reactions to the revivals can be found in the number of persons participating in the activities. To get people to engage actively in religious work was Moody's dominant aim. That many persons took part has already been observed in earlier portions of this study. A single example should serve our purpose here. The number of persons taking part in the New York services in 1876 is indicative. Fifty persons were on the committee in charge of the meetings; 1,200 were trained for the choir; 500 were trained as ushers; 225 were specially trained to handle the converts at the end of each meeting. Added to these were the people distributing the thousands of tickets to special meetings, holding various auxiliary meetings, handling advertising, passing out handbills, visiting saloons and billiard parlors to invite all to come to the meetings, and engaging in the systemized house to house canvas. . . .[5]

These were some of the more immediate results. About

some of the longer range and more permanent results of the Moody revivals, Huber has this to say:

> There are additional factors in Moody's life, however, which reveal a desire to bring greater permanence to the work he was doing. Although he believed that it was essential to get people "stirred up," and though he spent the winter months in revival services, more and more of his energies were directed toward other activities. These were the founding and development of the Northfield Seminary for girls, the Mount Hermon School for boys, the Northfield Summer Bible Conferences, the Bible Institute for Home and Foreign Missions, and the Colportage Library Publications. In a sense, these institutions were testaments to Moody's ability to persuade. . . .
>
> Moody was responsible for two important changes in the course of revivalism. The first of these changes arose from his main theme, that God was a God of love. Prior to Moody, the great emphasis of evangelists was on a wrathful God and the awfulness of hell. Revivalists before Moody had preached the compassion and love of God, but they had not emphasized it. . . .
>
> The second change that Moody wrought was the introduction of methods of organization and administration that were deliberately aimed toward developing an urban community into a psychological crowd in order to facilitate conversions and active participation in religious endeavors. Prior to this time many revival audiences had been transformed into psychological crowds, but never before had methods of business been introduced; never had tabernacles been built in successive cities; never had there been such deliberate and widespread planning.[6]

The public address critic can immediately discern in the above that his analyses can be comprised of social and religious as well as rhetorical components, that the results can sometimes have far-ranging impacts. All this suggests the significance of rhetoric and public address in the development of a society.

Other scholars, too, see this influence. Others also have an abiding interest in the influence of significant speakers and the results of their speechmaking. Such a one is Clarence Mondale, American Studies scholar at the University of Alabama. Writing in a recent issue of the

American Quarterly on "Daniel Webster and Technology," Mondale indicates that his aim is to "limit our discussion to what Webster said about technology and its public consequences."[7] His essay is a content analysis of a number of speeches of Webster that bear on industry, manufacturing, and labor. The effects found by Mondale are not as specific as the ones of Robert B. Huber in his work on Dwight L. Moody. Concerned as Mondale is with the larger cultural context of speechmaking, the conclusions he reaches are quite different. They suggest that Webster's role as a great orator, at least in his concern with technology, was one of a practical and powerful kind of popular education. More specifically, he indicates that Webster succeeded in his aim of making technology a suitable subject for public discourse; the consequences of Webster's orations then were a revelation to the American public.[8]

Still another kind of effect and influence of speeches is shown by Dallas C. Dickey and Donald C. Streeter in their study of Lucius Q. C. Lamar. They point out the effects of Lamar's speaking in two ways. About a single speech, a eulogy on Calhoun, they say:

> One speech, "John C. Calhoun—His Life, Character, and Public Services", delivered at the unveiling of a monument in honor of the South Carolinian, at Charleston, April 26, 1887, was among the most important of his life. Although the address, lengthy and philosophical in nature, has been largely relegated to oblivion in the days since its delivery, its importance cannot be overlooked. As Frederick Jackson Turner evolved and expressed in subsequent years his frontier theory of American history, he referred to Lamar's speech for support and evidence: . . . Whether Lamar's influence on Turner was great or small, Turner's citation is noteworthy for his appreciation of the manner in which Lamar demonstrated and expressed broad evolutionary concepts of American history in the Calhoun address.[9]

The long range influence of another Lamar speech, that of the eulogy on Charles Sumner, is seen in the following:

> If one wishes for a tangible manifestation of the recognition and influence of speaking, one may today view the

Peace Window in the Sigma Alpha Epsilon Temple at Evanston, Illinois, which was inspired by Lamar's eulogy on Sumner. The window which pictures Christ in the center and a Union and Confederate soldier on each side, is a forceful reminder of the philosopher, dreamer, and statesman whose career ran concurrently with the expansion of the Deep South, the civil struggle for the essential features of its genteel agrarianism, and the convulsive aftermath of the war—reconstruction and reconciliation.[10]

In their conclusion, Dickey and Streeter evaluate in general terms the total impact of the speaking of this great son of the South. They say:

The immediate effect of Lamar's speeches was favorable. Opponents, including congressional contemporaries, such as Blaine and Hoar, were moved to admiration. Newspapers from coast to coast reprinted his speeches either in part or in their entirety, with complimentary editorial comment. The audiences present were often large and responsive. He received more requests for public speeches than he was able to fill. He delivered outstanding public addresses to the New York Chamber of Commerce, and at the unveiling of the statue of Calhoun. From time to time he spoke also at commencement exercises at some educational institution, notably Emory University.[11]

These few excerpts should illustrate some of the analytical approaches that can be used to measure the results of speechmaking of various kinds. The critic of public address can use these as springboards to his own creative activity in this realm of assessment. It would be easier for him to emulate these approaches. Manifestly, this would not only not be enough but would probably be an error. It would be an error because it would limit his potential, and in fact undermine his moves toward fulfilling his own creative probings and possibilities. Where possible, the critic should look for methods that would provide unique assessments, assessments in depth of the speaker's impact upon specific audiences as well as upon his times. This is the least that he can do as an efficacious scholar and critic.

While assessment of the effects of speechmaking is of paramount importance, not every analytical study must focus on this area. Fewer do now than has been the case in the past. Perhaps the doctrine so popular with some rhetorical scholars—that too much emphasis upon the favorable results of a speech may lead to an unhealthy resurgence of sophistic theory—can be the cause for the decline of this kind of evaluation. Whatever the reason, it behooves speech critics to spend some time, at least, on this interesting aspect of analysis and interpretation. If public address is wedded to ideas, if its practice is a functional one in society, if, in short, the practice of public address is part and parcel of a democratic society, playing its role in the changes and development of that society, then the results, effects, and ramifications of the speeches and speakers need to be ascertained. The public address critic could do worse than to look to the results of the speeches, past and present, as a way to fulfill the above aim.

QUESTIONS AND PROJECTS

1. Write a short paper delineating the criteria you would use to determine the results of a persuasive political speech; an informative, intellectual one; a eulogy; a sermon.

2. Examine the essays in Volume III of the *History and Criticism of American Public Address*. How many of them are concerned in some way with the results of the speech-making? Select one essay that does not perform this function and write a paper indicating how you believe the study would be strengthened if such an analysis of the orator's speeches were made.

3. Follow a similar process with Volume I of the *History and Criticism*, and with Volume II.

4. Evaluate the effects of Booker T. Washington's "Atlanta Exposition Address" upon his immediate audience and his time. What effects has this address had upon our own time? What effects has it had in the South? In the North?

5. Write a short paper analyzing and interpreting the value of Henry Grady's "The New South" upon the position of the South after the Civil War. Do the same for the position of the North.
6. Write a critical study evaluating the effects of former President Dwight D. Eisenhower's Inaugural Address in 1952 upon his subsequent administration. Do a similar study with the 1956 Inaugural Address.
7. What value for our time has Thomas Jefferson's First Inaugural Address had? What were its function and results upon his own time?

NOTES

1. Richard H. Rovere, "Letter from Washington," *The New Yorker* (April 11, 1964), pp. 149–155.
2. ———, "The Minds of Barry Goldwater," *Harper's Magazine*, 229, 1372 (September, 1964), 37–42.
3. Quoted in A. Craig Baird, *American Public Addresses 1740–1952* (New York: McGraw-Hill, 1956), p. 116.
4. Robert B. Huber, "Dwight L. Moody," in *History and Criticism of American Public Address*, Marie Hochmuth, ed. (New York: Russell & Russell, Publishers, 1955), Vol. III, pp. 252–253.
5. *Ibid.*, pp. 254–255.
6. *Ibid.*, pp. 257–258.
7. Clarence Mondale, "Daniel Webster and Technology," *American Quarterly*, XIV, 1 (Spring, 1962), p. 38.
8. *Ibid.*, pp. 46–47.
9. Dallas C. Dickey and Donald C. Streeter, "Lucius Q. C. Lamar," in *History and Criticism of American Public Address*, Marie Hochmuth, ed., *op. cit.*, p. 212.
10. *Ibid.*, p. 217.
11. *Ibid.*, pp. 217–218.

SELECTED BIBLIOGRAPHY

Baird, A. Craig, ed., *American Public Addresses: 1740–1952,* New York: McGraw-Hill, 1956.
Dickey, Dallas C. and Donald C. Streeter, "Lucius Q. C.

Lamar," in *History and Criticism of American Public Address,* Marie Hochmuth, ed., New York: Russell & Russell, Publishers, 1955, Vol. III.

Howell, Wilbur Samuel and Hoyt Hopewell Hudson, "Daniel Webster," in *History and Criticism of American Public Address,* William N. Brigance, ed., New York: McGraw-Hill, 1943, Vol. II.

Huber, Robert B., "Dwight L. Moody," in *History and Criticism of American Public Address,* Marie Hochmuth, ed., *op. cit.*

Mondale, Clarence, "Daniel Webster and Technology," *American Quarterly,* XIV, 1 (Spring, 1962), 37–47.

Thonssen, Lester and A. Craig Baird, *Speech Criticism,* New York: Ronald Press, 1948, Chapter 17.

Utterback, William E., "Contemporary Theories of Public Opinion," *Studies in Speech and Drama in Honor of Alexander M. Drummond,* Ithaca; Cornell University Press, 1944.

Vorys, John M., "How a Member of Congress Measures the Response of his Constituents," *Quarterly Journal of Speech,* XXXII, 2 (April, 1946), 170–172.

Wrage, Ernest J. and Barnet Baskerville, eds., *Contemporary Forum,* New York: Harper & Row, 1962.

Part Two.

Intrinsic Factors
in the Criticism
of Public Address

5 Historical Description and Analysis of the Speaker's Ideas

The material that has appeared thus far in this book has been concerned with factors outside the speech, whether the speech is viewed as an aesthetic document or a functional craftsmanlike one, or both. The critic of public address has learned that he must have an abiding interest not only in the artistic and functional aspects of rhetoric and public address, but in biography, history, philosophy, politics, psychology, religion, and sociology. The following chapters deal more with the speech itself, or the intrinsic factors as they are called here. The material will include the above disciplines as well as other significant ones such as literature and logic. To be sure, it is easy to see that the critic of public address needs the disciplinary approach of rhetoric as the first and most important requisite in his analyses and assessments. By now it should also be as easy to see that the utilization of the interdisciplinary approach to the above-named fields is almost equally important. In short, the critic should give special attention to the whole field of American studies. American studies is a broad interdisciplinary view of the totality of American culture. This framework is used rather than the procedure of one field, no matter how important that particular field may be.

So the beginning of this section, concerned with ideas, concepts, and issues with which a speaker has become identified, illustrates again that broad spectrum of disciplines within which the speech critic needs to move in a facile fashion. For when we speak of ideas, we speak of concepts which have philosophical, intellectual, religious, political, or social precedents and ramifications. The primary concern of this chapter is the study of the speaker's beliefs and philosophy; in short, what the speaker stands for.

The discussion, however, will necessarily include both extrinsic and intrinsic factors. In essence this will be a transitional chapter, since insights into a speaker's beliefs must involve an understanding of the man himself. The critic must view those extrinsic factors concerning the man, his life and the development of his ideas in relation to the philosophy presented in a speech.

There are many reasons for representing accurately the ideas of a particular speaker in a critical study, even if those views never appear explicitly in the orator's oral discourse. It is most important to provide a full and meaningful comprehension of the man and his character. It is necessary, therefore, first to discern what kind of an ideologist the speaker was. Was he a conservative, a liberal, a middle-of-the-roader, a reformer? If he were none of these, although this is rather difficult to imagine, was he a pragmatist, a realist, an opportunist, or a compromiser, to mention but a few of the possibilities.

Intellectual historians, social philosophers, political theorists, and sociologists, from the point of view of their own disciplines, can often contribute useful discernments into a speaker's concepts. While the public address critic should scrutinize these, he should use them only as a point of departure for his own descriptions and analyses of his subject's views and concepts. The contributions of scholars in other disciplines can also be useful because of the methodology used. A historian, for example, will probably examine the total work of a person, speeches, addresses, essays, political writings, even diaries and journals, before offering his own conclusions.

Arthur M. Schlesinger, Jr., illustrates the above point in his celebrated studies of Andrew Jackson and Franklin D. Roosevelt. The speech critic could find the Schlesinger analyses quite helpful, provided that the critic takes into account Schlesinger's own somewhat subjective predilections toward the object of his biography. While some material in Schlesinger's studies involves interpretation and evaluation, much of it is historical and factual description. When Schlesinger points out, for instance, the basic ideas contained in Franklin D. Roosevelt's early speech given at Troy, New York, on March 4, 1912, on the role, responsibility, development, and conservation of society, the public address critic can find material useful to his own scrutiny of Roosevelt's growth as a speaker.[1] Then, if a comparison is made with Roosevelt's "Commonwealth Club Address"[2] given two decades later, the critic can discover that the wellsprings of Roosevelt's ideas did not develop overnight. He can also perceive that Roosevelt was not always the realistic pragmatist he has been considered, but an individual with a personal philosophy which was being developed over a long period of time. His commitment to such ideas had significant consequences, not only for Roosevelt, but also for the United States.

While the above details might be considered descriptive, or factual historical material, a germ of analysis also pervades this kind of examination. This is so because on the analytical level, there is constantly an attempt to understand why a person believed and stood for certain ideas. In the case of Franklin D. Roosevelt, for example, one could well ask what were the specific factors that led him to embrace the ideas and philosophy which he held. This, to be sure, would involve the critical undertaking discussed in the previous chapter—that of the biographical data dealing with the individual. It may be found that certain experiences led Roosevelt to espouse his particular creed. Some analysts have suggested that Roosevelt's aristocratic upbringing, his aristocratic mien, his concept of stewardship, and his bout with polio as a young man all had a great deal to do with his ideological development. The critic's job here is really cut out for him. It is not a simple process to unearth this kind of data. It is even more difficult to show its relationship to the speaker's views.

There is the additional task of analyzing the results of a particular social philosophy of an individual, not only to discern its origins, but also its effects. In scrutinizing the speaker's life, the analyst needs to ask whence came the beliefs and wherein do they lead.

Ideas and concepts, too, are not held in a vacuum, although some abstract thinkers and philosophers, or perhaps metaphysicians, may be able to do this. Not so with the orator. Since his ideas are ingredients for speech-making, the sources for his primary activity, they are often tied to the major issues of his time. Another specific purpose, then, of the critical rhetorical scholar, once he has determined what the speaker stood for at a certain juncture, is to examine these views more closely and comprehensively with the aim of perceiving and disclosing how they were welded into a program for action. This kind of exegesis can bear fruitful results.

Consider John C. Calhoun's concept of Greek Democracy. According to some scholars, Calhoun was reputed to have held his point of view during the last stages of his own lifetime. It may be obvious to students of the pre-Civil War scene that there are salient relationships of this ideal to the hierarchically structured society which was operative in the South, and whose continued existence Calhoun advocated so ably in speech and essay in his later years. Perhaps these significant relationships are the similarities between the Greek Democracy, especially that of Athens and Calhoun's beloved South. Both were built on a solid foundation of slavery: the Greeks with their war captives and the South with the Negro. Both believed in an aristocratic ruling body, even though this was to be arrived at through an emasculated version of democratic procedures. Plato's *Republic,* in a way, served as a mentor for the Greeks and the Southerners. Neither believed in a fluid and dynamic social structure. Both were committed to a constitutionally static one, which allows only a modicum of change, if any. It is significant that both civilizations declined and fell partially because of these factors. These are some of the obvious similarities which a student of criticism can rather easily discern.

But what of the differences? Are there salient ones that the scholar may indicate which would not make this analogy a good one? Are the following differences pertinent? The encroachment of the industrial revolution from the North and its impact upon the South and its civilization? The great size of the South, with its resultant political and social difficulties as compared with the small Greek city states? The lack of an intellectual elite in the South, and the lack of educational facilities to educate such an elite, as compared with Athens, for example? These differences may prevent the analogy from being fully valid. It could be the aim of the critic of public address to unearth and dissect these conditions and factors, not only as a prelude to a study of Calhoun's speechmaking, but perhaps as a value in itself.

That a study of a speaker's philosophy by a rhetorician can have intrinsic value, even though it is not a prelude to a critical rhetorical analysis as such, has been demonstrated often. One of the early works in this domain is Robert T. Oliver's tri-part study of Webster, Clay and Calhoun, which appeared in the *Quarterly Journal of Speech*.[3] Using a variety of historical materials, Oliver presents in a facile fashion the motivating ideas and ideals of these three greats of "The Golden Age of American Oratory."

The critic who attempts to understand the speaker's beliefs and to use them in a reciprocal manner has indeed a challenging task. This process, first of having the person's ideas used in clarifying his speeches, and second the invention within the speeches used to illustrate his ideas, is most effectively used by the scholar if he utilizes the vast amount of material available to him. Simple examples immediately come to mind. No scrutiny of Alexander Hamilton or James Madison as a speaker really would be quite complete without the utilization in some way of Hamilton's or Madison's contributions to *The Federalist* papers. This would be particularly true if the invention of these two, by way of comparison and contrast, were to be the object of the dissection.

Private papers also can often shed light on a speaker's social, intellectual, religious, or political views. Ralph Waldo Emerson was a tremendously popular lecturer who left a large legacy of his ideas in his speeches and addresses. These, to be sure, must be examined for an understanding of his philosophy of transcendentalism. But even here the fuller comprehension, analysis, and eventual evaluation of Emerson's views can be enhanced by a careful reading of his *Journals*. His poetry, too, if it is carefully studied, can aid in that regard.

Of course it is not uncommon for rhetorical critics to look to more private sources such as journals and diaries for fuller cognition of a speaker's beliefs. But very few, if any, rhetorical critics—or literary critics, for that matter—have attempted the study and relationship of a person's poetry and his rhetoric. This is unfortunate, because as almost any rhetorical scholar knows, there are some interesting and useful discernments to be made in the comparison and contrast of the latter two disciplines. These can be concerned with both content and structure. One need only look to those two epoch-making studies of Charles Sears Baldwin, *Ancient Rhetoric and Poetic* and *Medieval Rhetoric and Poetic*, for examples of this process. Emerson, quite obviously, is not the only individual who could be analyzed in this way. Walt Whitman is another. There are extant lectures of this poet which might prove helpful in many ways for an understanding, not only of his poetry, but of the man himself, as well as of his views.

In dealing with the ideas of an orator, the critic of public address is confronted with difficulties. The omnipresent one, quite obviously, is the problem of obtaining materials dealing objectively with the speaker's viewpoints. While the problem is present in working with almost any individual, be he philosopher, thinker, theologian, or writer, the difficulty is compounded in the case of an orator. While it may not be as hard with a speaker who confines his speaking to the realm of the intellect as Ralph Waldo Emerson, or the religious, as Harry Emerson Fosdick, it is more manifest in the case of a successful politician such as Abraham Lincoln or Theodore Roosevelt.

It is less difficult in the first instance because the speaker is more concerned with universal values than with the transient problems of the moment. It is more difficult in the second instance because the very fibre of the life of a politician, and hence the very fabric of his speeches, is to deal with the problems of change in a society. This happens as the people move from one viewpoint to another, now conservative, now liberal, now even radical. If the speaker-politician is to survive in this dynamic jungle of politics, he must adjust to the many exigencies of the particular situation. As a result, certain values and virtues which he holds dear will need to be modified, or he will rapidly be relegated to private life.

Then there is the further leavening influence, in many cases, of the speaker-politician's own success. The responsibilities of office have often caused a modification of views. What may have looked like a simple problem from the outside, to be solved within the framework of the individual's ideology, is then discovered—from the inside—to be a monumental one in which many factors need to be considered. The simplistic approach just will not do. The politician discovers that to give simple answers to complex questions is the epitome of naiveté, and may lead to tragic results. Senator Barry Goldwater, for instance, had been accused of this early in the 1964 presidential campaign by Senator Hubert H. Humphrey, the Democratic vice-presidential candidate, and by fellow Republicans. Goldwater modified his views somewhat as the campaign progressed, perhaps because of the accusations, bringing them more in keeping with moderate ideals. There is little doubt that as a result of such factors, the politician's rhetoric is affected.

Most often, as a society changes its views, so will the orator-politician. This will be reflected in his speech-making. Again Abraham Lincoln can serve as a prime example. Excerpts from his speeches, ostensibly indicating his views on many subjects, have been quoted by capitalist as well as Communist. Evaluations of his ideas by historian, political scientist, sociologist, or rhetorician place him as an anti-slavery man, or a pro-slavery man, an egalitarian, or an anti-egalitarian. Whom is the public address critic, searching for truth, to believe in the final analysis? Obviously no one completely, but the speaker himself (in his own works) and the critic's own judgment of the speaker.

While it is useful for the purpose of analysis to look at divergent views of a speaker's ideas, this is only the introduction to the critic's own scrutiny. This kind of weighing and evaluating is the very foundation of the critic's responsibility. In addition to examining other views of the speaker's values and the speaker's own documents (such as diaries, journals, essays, letters, and the like), the public address critic has one other major resource.

This major resource is an analysis of the speaker's actions in relation to his words. Are these actions congruent with the ideology expressed in the person's speechmaking? Do the actions implement his concepts and values, or do they work at cross purposes? While it is almost a truism to say that theory and practice do not mix—as indeed often they do not—this does not mean that an individual's rhetoric may not contain certain injunctions which if carried to fruition will result in certain consequences. What are these consequences? How do they reflect the speaker's attitude toward life? How, in fact, from the critic's point of view, do ideas and consequences reflect his character? This, as has been seen in an earlier chapter, ideas, actions, and consequences of these actions inevitably do. These are only some of the hard questions that the critic needs to ask himself, and indeed answer for himself, if he is to make useful analyses of the speaker's ideas and philosophy as a prelude to evaluation and criticism.

A recent monograph on Thomas Jefferson's speaking, for example, makes use of some of the above critical procedure by attempting to answer some of the questions posed. The study is concerned with a series of relatively unknown addresses by Jefferson to American Indian audiences given while he was President of the United States. The conclusion of the work attempts to synthesize some of the factors involved into a meaningful summary. In the process, some new discernments into Jefferson as person and persuader are given:

This case study of a set of addresses in which ideas changed sharply and in which the word of one period was not the deed of the next has significant implications regarding both politics generally and Jefferson specifically.

1. When practical pressures conflict with individual ideals so directly that no accommodation is possible, policies are likely to coincide with the pressures. That such was the outcome in the case of Thomas Jefferson, a man with strong democratic convictions, lends strength to such a generalization. If a man of his moral and political strength could not withstand the call of expediency, expecting idealistic conduct from politicians generally seems a false hope.

2. The usual picture of Jefferson as a consummate democrat should be reevaluated. In his dealings with the Indians his words and deeds did not coincide, and his general position as an advocate of equality was breached.

3. Jefferson was more inclined to use the persuasive process and more skillful in its employment than has been believed in the past. In dealing with the Indians he adapted intelligently to occasion and audience, employed his ethical advantages skillfully, showed good judgment in arrangement and in control over length, and combined logical and emotional appeals with a shrewd view to his true long-range objectives. Finally, he played skillfully on the nuance values of words as his own policies and corresponding speech purposes were altered.

These three points suggest a need for moralizing and evaluating. Although it is somewhat true that "No historian has a right to be peeved with history, no student of political history has a right to be peeved when a politician says one thing and does another" the rhetorical critic should not be so easily satisfied.

Moral standards should be part of the critical apparatus; and if they are, Jefferson must be condemned for being less than consistent when his words to the redmen are compared with his actions. Our conception of his *ethos*, then, should be revised. The shifting position of Jefferson here is not consistent with the stalwart democratic image which in his own time and in our present day adds so much to the impact of his pronouncements.

Fallibility marks the relationship of his actions to his words; the high *ethos* stemming from his democratic spirit has not been entirely justified.

What Jefferson loses in stature as an idealist, he possibly makes up as a practical orator using invention, style, and presentation in the service of practical political ends. After this analysis of the addresses to the Indians, perhaps the proper appellation for Jefferson is "Thomas Jefferson: The Idealist as Realist."[4]

Many rhetorical studies of individual speakers contain the more usual delineation of an orator's views. Fortunately for the budding public address critic, some of these sources are readily available. He can examine these to see how other rhetorical critics go about this task of describing and analyzing the credos of important and seminal speakers. He can look at Orville A. Hitchcock's interesting exegesis of the religious ideas of Jonathan Edwards, the Colonial Puritan. Hitchcock states:

> . . . Jonathan Edwards was a strict Calvinist, an arch-conservative in an age that was becoming increasingly liberal in theological ideas. He was a true Congregationalist, who adhered to the doctrines of the vigorous theology of more than a century before. His philosophy had its beginnings in the works of Calvin. He taught the religion of the first generation of Puritans, when the spirit of Congregationalism was strong and dynamic. In the days of a lowering of standards and a lessening of restrictions Jonathan Edwards stood out as a successful defender of strict Calvinistic orthodoxy. Because of his influence, and that of others like him, the older Calvinism had one great final flare-up before it died out almost completely.
>
> It must be noted, however, that there runs through Edwards' sermons a more profound strain of mysticism and pathos than is to be found in the works of most of his orthodox predecessors. Edwards set forth the Congregational theology in all its grimness, but he went beyond the other ministers in the emphasis of complete inner conversion and in the addition of human appeal to the traditional severely logical theology. As John Fiske says, "The distinction between the converted and the unconverted became in his hands more vitally important than the older distinction between the elect and the non-elect." It was this holding forth of the possibility of conversion that set the stage for the great revivals which developed from Edwards' preaching.
>
> What were the doctrines which Edwards preached? Analysis of his sermons reveals that eight fundamental

theological tenets form the basis of his theology. He taught (1) that the entire truth of religion is contained in the Holy Scriptures; (2) that man is a lowly, mean creature, tainted with the guilt of Adam's sin; (3) that man is completely and universally dependent upon God; (4) that the invisible church is composed of a small number of elect, who will continue to be saints throughout eternity; (5) that these elect become aware that they are saints through divine revelation in conversion; (6) that for the elect the practice of true religion is "sweet" and "pleasant"; (7) that the remainder of mankind are doomed to eternal suffering, which they can escape in part through prayer and repentance, partaking in a sort of "common grace"; and, finally, (8) that God is sovereign and supreme.

These eight principles, aside from the emphasis on common grace, were fundamental to the strictest Calvinism. They were the principles that had motivated the establishment of the congregational Church. Theoretically, the church still clung to these tenets, but, actually, by Edwards' time, Arminianism had made great inroads. Arminianism had a more optimistic tone than Calvinism. It made the admission requirements to the church less strict (conversion was not required); it offered more hope to the sinner (anyone could be saved); it gave man more faith in himself (man had a certain freedom of will); it permitted a more passive moral attitude; and it affirmed that saints could fall from grace. Calvinism was doomed to give way to it. That it held on as long as it did was due partly to the speaking and writing of Jonathan Edwards.[5]

As far as political ideas are concerned, the student of speech criticism has many sources. Notable among these is Norman C. Mattis' description of the values held by Thomas Hart Benton. Mattis says:

Benton's leading ideas, and the position he occupied in our national life may be conveniently though incompletely summarized under four headings. He was (1) a radical democrat, (2) a Westerner, (3) an expansionist, and (4) a Unionist.

1. A Jeffersonian democrat in the equalitarian rather than the State-rights line of descent, Benton had unwavering faith in the wisdom of the people. In his old age he wrote of their "instinctive sagacity . . . which is an over-match for book learning; and which being disinterested, is always

honest." Thirty years earlier, about the time Harriet Martineau was contemptuously calling him a "temporary People's man" whom nature had designed to be a barber, he told the Senate that "the body of the people are always sincerely devoted to the interests of their country, and their honest mistakes are less dangerous to liberty than may be the artful designs of a small and select body." The United States, he added, had demonstrated the great moral truth, that "under a free Government, the power of the intellect is the only power which rules the affairs of men; and virtue and intelligence the only passports to honor and preferment." The people may be temporarily misled or thwarted by the force or fraud of powerful minorities, but in the long run the judgment of the majority will be right and must prevail. Perhaps as Theodore Roosevelt said, Benton rode loose in the saddle when on his democratic hobby. . . .

2. Though not a native of the West, Benton made himself the special guardian of that vast region. In return, as Senator Sevier remarked, the Westerners named their counties, their towns, and their children for him. He knew the immensity and richness of our empty spaces, and believed that nothing but an illiberal land policy could hinder the rise of great commonwealths in the Mississippi Valley. . . . He sponsored measures to mark and protect the road to Santa Fe, to abolish the Indian Factory System, to fortify the Oregon Trail, to legalize the Spanish and French land grants, to construct a highway to the Pacific, and to do a dozen other constructive things. The Western outlook also gave impetus, edge, and urgency to many Bentonian measures, such as reform of the land system and abolition of the salt duties, that in a more fundamental sense were part of the general Jacksonian economic program.

3. As an expansionist or imperialist and early disciple of the doctrine of manifest-destiny, Benton read history as the march of the white race westward, with the Anglo-Saxons in the vanguard. The Americans spearheaded the Anglo-Saxons, and to maintain American primacy he would fight our British comrades-in-destiny as readily as he would fight the lesser breeds. . . . Jingoistic he sometimes sounded, but he never urged a militant front unless convinced that we had superior claim in both law and equity. . . .

4. Benton was a Unionist who set himself against all separatist tendencies from the moment he recognized, rather tardily, the implications of the South Carolina doctrine of

nullification. Adopting as his formula for slavery "no extension and no agitation" he opposed both the abolitionists and the Southern extremists, who were alike in placing their special values above the Union, and who, like the two halves of a pair of shears, could not cut until joined together. From 1835 on he thought of the South, and especially of John C. Calhoun, as the aggressors. On February 18, 1847, when Calhoun, presented his resolutions asserting that Congress had no power to bar slavery from the territories, Benton promptly labeled them "firebrand." Calhoun observed that he had expected to find the representative of a slave state on his side. "I shall be found in the right place—on the side of my country and the Union," retorted Benton. When his state legislature instructed him to vote for the resolutions or their equivalent, he "appealed from the instructions," waged a campaign on the issue, and went down in defeat; but twelve years later, when Missouri by a narrow margin remained within the Union, his lingering influence played an important part.

To define Benton as a democrat, a Westerner, an expansionist, and a Unionist is not, of course, to explain him fully or to account for his position on all the issues that a senator of 1820–1850 had to meet. It was, however, by his attempts to extend economic and political democracy, to foster the development of the West, to expand the country to its present continental dimensions, and to preserve the United States as an indivisible whole, that he made his greatest impact upon the nation.[6]

The student of public address criticism can see from these few excerpts the divergent roads that can be taken by the critic in explaining the orator's basic ideas. The studies can focus on political or religious views, or the total corpus of a speaker's philosophy; or they can emphasize one concept or idea which motivated the speaker. This latter is shown in a study of "Frances Wright: Egalitarian Reformer." Wright was the prominent woman orator of the Jacksonian period whose platform appearances opened up the speaker's rostrum to the weaker sex. Her ideas on the egalitarian ideal, gleaned from speech and essay, can be summarized as follows:

It is no exaggeration to say that up to her time in America, and in fact for some generations after, nowhere in the utterance of any individual has there been such an understanding and advocacy of equalitarianism as in the speaking of Frances Wright. Taking her cue from the Declaration of Independence as a basic philosophy, she sought to implement the generalizations of that document by making them into specific propositions and even into actualities. This action was to be accomplished both practically and philosophically.

From the practical viewpoint, the accomplishment would take place by making education equally available to all; a statewide system of schools sponsored by the government was to be the instrument to attain this end. Only in this fashion could the inequalities be abolished and true equality reign. Unique also was her advocacy not only of equal education for women, but also of considering them the equals of men in all endeavor as well as in the social and intellectual milieu. Only in this way could equality for all be accomplished.

From the philosophical view, too, Wright brought to bear new insights about equalitarian doctrine. A true Republic, such as the Americans ostensibly aspired to, she thought, needed the foundation of equality for its proper functioning. Equality too, was essential to liberty; there could not be liberty for the few, until there was liberty for all.

Frances Wright was far ahead of her time in calling for a more equalitarian society through the means of more equal instruction for both men and women. That many of the ideas themselves have taken concrete form is evidenced in the greater equality of suffrage for women, and in the widespread system of public schools and colleges disseminating more nearly equally the knowledge necessary for a better functioning of our democracy. Thus the egalitarian ideal that was espoused by Wright, spawned during the rise of the common man, helped to set in motion those practical forces which have aided in making our society what it is today.[7]

While the study of the ideas of a speaker usually functions as only one part of a full scale study, this same research and scrutiny may have other objectives. Not the least among the aims is the examination and delineation of a speaker's concepts as a value in itself. It has been a continuing assumption in this book that the public address critic is not to study speeches or speakers alone, although this is probably his first job. But there should be nothing preventing the scholar well versed in rhetoric, as well as in some of the other disciplines such as intellectual history, literature, or theology, to make distinct and unique contributions in other ways. If his main interest is in ideas, then he would do well to study the concepts of significant orators. Ideas are too important to leave to the intellectual historian or philosopher alone. They are, to be sure, the very "stuff" of rhetoric. Thus the rhetorician should indeed make his own valid contributions and assessments.

Nor should the critic of public address be frightened by the assertions of some rhetorical scholars that the critic would do well to leave ideas alone, that they are not in his domain. In the same manner that a critic can concern himself with the historical background, the audience and occasion, the biography of a speaker, or the effects of the speeches as the central aim of his work, so too can he make the center of his study the ideas and values of a speaker.

QUESTIONS AND PROJECTS

1. Write a short paper on the relationship of Ralph Waldo Emerson's transcendentalism to his address, "The American Scholar" or to his "Divinity School Address."
2. In what way did Theodore Parker use his concepts of society to delineate his religious views in his sermons? His social views in lectures?
3. Transcendentalism was influential in the thought and speech of both Emerson and Parker. Write a short paper showing this influence on their religious views. Compare and contrast these views.
4. What politico-philosophic premises underlie the speaking of the following:

Abraham Lincoln	Susan B. Anthony
Stephen A. Douglas	Ignatius Donnelly
James G. Blaine	Herbert Hoover
Robert G. Ingersoll	Richard M. Nixon

5. What is the relation of logical proof to political philosophy? What is its relation to theology? Write a paper developing these ideas.
6. Take any successful political speaker, such as William E. Borah or William Jennings Bryan, and write an account delineating his social views, as expressed in speeches and writings, and his political actions. Were they congruent? If not, why not?
7. What facets of rhetoric are used by Richard Hofstadter in his analyses of prominent figures in his *The American Political Tradition?*
8. What facets of rhetoric are used by Arthur M. Schlesinger, Jr., in his work, *The Age of Jackson?*

NOTES

1. For an exposition of this speech see, Arthur M. Schlesinger, Jr., *The Crisis of the Old Order* (Boston: Houghton, Mifflin, 1957), pp. 336–338.
2. For text of the address see, Ernest J. Wrage and Barnet Baskerville, eds., *Contemporary Forum* (New York: Harper & Row, 1962), pp. 146–156.
3. Robert T. Oliver, "Behind the Word: Studies in the Political and Social Views of the Slave-Struggle Orators," *Quarterly Journal of Speech*, XXII, 3 (October, 1936), 413–429; XXIII, 1 (February, 1937), 13–32; XXIII, 3 (October, 1937), 409–426.
4. Anthony Hillbruner, "Word and Deed: Jefferson's Addresses to the Indians," *Speech Monographs*, XXX, 4 (November, 1963), 333–334.
5. Orville A. Hitchcock, "Jonathan Edwards," in *History and Criticism of American Public Address*, William N. Brigance, ed. (New York: McGraw-Hill, 1943), Vol. I, pp. 220–222. I have omitted Hitchcock's copious documentation for these conclusions. The documentation illustrates the pain that the scholar takes to be sure his analysis and interpretations are valid and reliable.
6. Norman C. Mattis, "Thomas Hart Benton," in *History and Criticism of American Public Address*, Marie Hochmuth, ed. (New York: Russell & Russell, Publishers, 1955), Vol. III, pp. 58–61.

7. Anthony Hillbruner, "Frances Wright: Egalitarian Reformer," *Southern Speech Journal*, XXIII, 4 (Summer, 1958), 203.

SELECTED BIBLIOGRAPHY

Auer, J. Jeffery, *An Introduction to Research in Speech*, New York: Harper & Row, 1950.

Baldwin, Charles Sears, *Ancient Rhetoric and Poetic*, New York: Macmillan, 1924.

———, *Medieval Rhetoric and Poetic*, New York: Macmillan, 1928.

Commager, Henry Steele, *The American Mind*, New Haven: Yale University Press, 1950.

Hillbruner, Anthony, "American Studies and Public Address," *Western Speech*, XXIV, 1 (Winter, 1960), 49–51.

———, "Inequality, The Great Chain of Being and Ante-Bellum Southern Oratory," *Southern Speech Journal*, XXV, 3 (Spring, 1960), 172–189.

Hofstadter, Richard, *The American Political Tradition*, New York: Alfred A. Knopf, 1948.

———, *The Age of Reform*, New York: Alfred A. Knopf, 1955.

Parrington, Vernon L., *Main Currents in American Thought*, New York: Harcourt, Brace, 1927.

Persons, Stow, *American Minds*, New York: Holt, Rinehart & Winston, 1958.

Schlesinger, Jr., Arthur M., *Age of Jackson*, Boston: Little, Brown, 1945.

———, *The Age of Roosevelt*, New York: Houghton, Mifflin, 1957, 1959, 1960, Vols. I, II, III.

Thonssen, Lester, and A. Craig Baird, *Speech Criticism*, New York: Ronald Press, 1948, Chapter 11.

6 Interpretation and Evaluation of the Speaker's Ideas

The previous chapter was concerned with the ideas of a speaker on the factual and descriptive level. But merely to state what a speaker believed, is not enough for public address criticism. The critic needs to go further; he needs to interpret and assess these ideas as a contribution to the criticism of public address, to culture and society, and hence to knowledge. While explication is an important aspect of criticism, the critic needs to show other factors. If he has talent, creativity, and intuition, these other factors will present a picture of the speaker which is a full portrait rather than a narrow profile. To see only one facet of a diamond is not enough for total comprehension and appreciation of its beauty. So, too, with the examination of a speaker and his ideas.

For a clearer understanding, an analogy from the art of painting might be helpful. Among the many techniques used by artists, two are the realistic and the surrealistic. The first one is relatively simple; the other more complex. A simple realistic painting of an individual, for example, will portray him full or three-quarter face, or perhaps in profile. It suggests the factual descriptive delineation of character and ideas. The more complex surrealistic one goes further. A surrealistic painting may contain full face and profile at one and the same time; it tries to depict the many facets of an individual, both external and internal. Applying this analogy to public address criticism means —as far as the speaker's ideas are concerned—that the scrutiny is at once descriptive, analytical, interpretative, synthetic, and evaluative. Only in this way can a full comprehension of the orator be gained. Therefore, at this level there is an attempt by the critic to wed description and analysis to interpretation and criticism. To use only one of these two major components in assessment is not enough.

In actuality, however, it is very difficult not to have at least a semblance of such a wedding. Writings, critiques, judgments most often do contain both elements. It is only for the purpose of clarity in analysis that these components are divided into two chapters in this book. In short, the lines between description and analysis on the one hand, and interpretation and criticism on the other, are somewhat artificial and arbitrary. Nevertheless, in explaining the theory of what the critic must do in practice, it is useful to have these boundaries.

But a constant injunction must be present. It is true that the critic must hold these differences between the simpler aspects of criticism (fact, analysis) and the more complicated ones (interpretation, assessment) in mind while he is doing his research and his thinking. But when he begins writing, maintaining this somewhat arbitrary distinction would only weaken and nullify the conclusions. For it is the welding of fact and criticism in writing which often produces the most lucid and striking and creative perceptions. This practice also makes far more interesting reading. If the critic merely follows a static critical format, he tends to bore the reader, who will see on every level where the critic is going. While this may not be tragic by itself, it does lessen critical impact. The great critical scholars and writers have creativity and use it.

There is the further problem of differentiating clearly between analysis and interpretation. It is true that the analysis and interpretation of ideas are closely allied, but interpretation is more closely tied to implication. Also the subjective element is present more in interpretation than in analysis. Ideological interpretation deals with both the indirect and overt meanings of the individual's ideas. Furthermore, this holds both for the immediate audience and for future society. Sometimes the implications and the indirect meaning of the ideas and views held by a speaker may have unplanned ramifications.

Consider the constitutional and social views of Alexander H. Stephens, the fiery southern orator and vice-president of the Confederacy. On one level, Stephens' ideas are the usual view of a southerner who may hide under the skirts of states' rights in order to preserve the magnolia and happy darky myth of the Old South. But to the student of ideas and their ramifications, other and perhaps more important implications and interpretations can be found. Such was a once popular idea, the concept of the "Great Chain of Being." This concept, which is a basis of most hierarchical societies, provides a philosophical rationale which the eloquent sons of the South certainly used.

The "Great Chain of Being" can be visualized by a picture of God the Creator and all his creation arranged in a divinely established hierarchical order. This order ranked in chain-like fashion from the Highest (that is, God) to the lowest form of sentient life. Each link had certain privileges and responsibilities appropriate to its rank. And all were linked together by reverence, piety, loyalty, and love. Thus, this concept fostered justice not by having everyone participate in it equally but according to his place in the hierarchy. In other words, justice was present in society when each man had those privileges and responsibilities appropriate to his rank and station.

That this idea had implications for the Old South is obvious. In studying the speechmaking and the ideas of Alexander H. Stephens, it has been discovered, for instance, that he forged "another link in that great divine process which had as its objective the maintenance of the South as the best of all possible worlds. . . ."[1] How was this done? Stephens accomplished it by focusing in his speeches upon two principles of the "Great Chain of Being," those of continuum and gradation. But what are these two principles? To explain this more thoroughly, we must go back to classical times.

The genesis of the idea in Greek philosophy comes from Plato who is the main historic source of other-worldliness, the foundation of the "Great Chain of Being." It is in his theory of Ideas that are found "the essences of all sorts of things which are paltry or ridiculous or even disgusting. So too in the actual world, since there needed to be sensible counterparts of every one of the Ideas."[2] This makes the created universe an exhaustive replica of the World of Ideas.

The World of Ideas stimulated the first principle of the "Great Chain," that of plenitude—the essential fullness of the sensible world; and in plenitude was based the second principle, that of continuity, which, however, came from Aristotle when he furnished posterity with a definition of the continuum: "Things are said to be continuous whenever there is one and the same limit of both wherein they overlap and which they possess in common."[3]

Aristotle also suggested the third principle known as gradation. Simply put, it meant "arranging all animals in a single graded *scala naturae* according to their degree of perfection,"[4] and ". . . each order possessing all the powers of those below it in the scale, and an additional differentiating one of its own."[5]

The synthesis of plenitude, continuity and gradation "was the plan and structure of the world . . . as a 'Great Chain of Being,' composed of an . . . infinite number of links ranging in hierarchical order from the meagerest kind of existence to . . . the Absolute Being."[6]

"Initially, this complex of ideas coming from Plato and Aristotle could only contribute in a nebulous way to the coherent general scheme of things that the "Great Chain of Being" became. Its evolution through the many stages of Neo-Platonism, of medieval thought, of its cosmological rationale in the sixteenth century finally culminated in its scientific sanction with the advent of Leibniz."[7]

Ultimately, however, it was the Age of Enlightenment which brought to fruition the principles of the "Chain" and used them "as weapons against social discontent and especially against all egalitarian movements."[8] Thus, when the nineteenth century Southerner utilized the concept to stifle equality, and sustain autocracy, he had a long philosophical tradition to uphold him. Even though [Stephens] . . . did not mention the "Great Chain," . . . this cosmological-social structure provided an important philosophical rationale for the institution of slavery in the South.[9]

The principle of continuity was implicit in the thought and speech of Alexander H. Stephens. The principle of gradation, however, was more explicitly developed.

Stephens, to be sure, would not extend the rights of liberty and equality to the colored race as he would to most whites.

Here a different principle operated, one which was known in antiquity, if Stephens is to be believed, but not utilized to its proper extent in the republics of old. Why it was not properly used and the results of this misuse of the Greek democratic idea were shown in the "Farewell Speech" of Stephens in 1859. These were the last words of Stephens in Congress prior to the Civil War, and they illustrate to what extent the South would go in establishing this great "truth," a "truth" which utilized one of the early principles of the "Great Chain," gradation, the *scala naturae* of Aristotle.[10]

Stephens eloquently indicated that:

Pythagoras, Plato and Aristotle, the greatest philosophers of antiquity directed their minds to the systems of government and the proper constitution of a State. The republican form was the ideal model of each. They all saw the necessity of some sort of *gradation* in the elements of its composition; but their systems failed, because *they violated nature* in not making the subordinate class of the negro. This great truth, that such was the normal condition of any race was not recognized in their theories; and hence their machinery, in practice could not work.[11]

The South, however, in the analysis of the future Vice-President of the Confederacy, did recognize this great new truth which came from nature. The hierarchical structure seen everywhere in nature was not to be violated; and practicalities, too, purposed toward that end.[12]

Stephens thus staunchly upheld the existent inequality and the hierarchically constructed society in the South as heaven-sent. Being, therefore, for the good of all, he thought, this caste society was not to be tampered with.[13]

The thinking and speaking of Stephens was thus part of that Southern dogma, based, inadvertently perhaps on the Aristotelian principles of continuum and gradation in the "Great Chain of Being"; but the chain was clearly seen when the dogma espoused inferiority and subservience for the Negro while at the same time advocating liberty and equality for the white man. This low link of the "Great

Chain," then, in Stephens' view, did not bind all men, but only the colored race.[14]

This comparison and relationship of Alexander H. Stephens and his social ideas to the "Great Chain of Being" is patently an individual interpretation. Nevertheless, it may have merit, not only for a truer and more vivid knowledge of Stephens, but for his fellow southern orators as well. In fact, these philosophical and social aspects of the concept illustrate and clarify not only the thinking of the old South, but today's thinking on social and racial problems as well. What is accomplished here is a discovery and delineation of new relationships, in this case between states' rights and the Negro problem on one side, and conservatism and hierarchical society on the other. Moreover, the critic should be aware that seeking new relationships is at the heart of new contributions and new knowledge. Little new knowledge springs full grown from a thinker's mind; most new contributions to thought are the result of seeing old ideas in a new light.

The above explanation and illustration of the interpretation of a philosophy, or point of view, of a prominent southern orator should indicate both the subjectivity and creativity in what might be called the level of social implications. But social implications of a person's ideas are not without their rhetorical implications, since the speaker used these as the foundation of speechmaking. This is material which the critic of public address needs.

The rhetorical implications of the interpretation of an orator's ideas do relate, then, to his subsequent speeches. They relate not only by invention, but they also relate by style and organization, and perhaps by other rhetorical criteria. Once certain ideas have been shown to have meaning in a speaker's life and oratorical output, they can be traced and interpreted when different issues arise. For example, how does the speaker deal rhetorically with attacks upon his cherished values? What does he do, from the standpoint either of logical or emotional proof, when the implications of his ideas are pointed out to him, perhaps by another talented speaker. Does he modify his views? Does he modify the actions coming from the views?

What of the influence of any of these possible changes upon his subsequent oratorical career? How does his language subsequently affect the ideas? What of the form of his addresses? What of other facets of structure in the speeches? Does the delivery of the speeches become modified in some way? These are but a few of the questions that a public address critic may ask himself when he looks at the speaker as an ideologue and attempts to interpret some of the rhetorical implications of the speaker's attitudes. These, then, are some of the omnipresent implications of the problem of interpretation. They, of course, are not easy to resolve.

Evaluation, the latter half of that interpretation-assessment duet considered in this chapter, is probably the most difficult. It is most difficult because it requires the most creative intuition, perception, and scholarship. The further the critic moves from the facts, the more he must depend on his own resources of reason and intuition. One could say, then, that evaluation or criticism is the most difficult of these processes because it is the least objective and scientific. It is the most subjective, artistic, and creative. It makes the critic most responsive and responsible to himself.

The critic, well aware of the subjectivity of individual judgment (even though solidly grounded in rhetorical theory), may be tempted to avoid a final commitment. This may be the reason why so few rhetorical critics today take that significant additional step beyond analysis: that of assessment. The critic, well-trained in rhetorical method and scholarship, might be nearly infallible in his description and analysis of rhetorical data. But he is aware that when he becomes a judge, using comparative methods in his critcism of men and their ideas, he becomes quite fallible. Here his rhetorical *accoutrements,* while to some degree strong enough to uphold him and his judgments, are not enough.

In what way, for example, can the public address critic use rhetorical tools exclusively in weighing and criticizing the speaker's ideas? This is a particularly difficult problem because in rhetoric as in literature a person's ideas are often held to be sacrosanct and, thus, not to be evaluated critically. A most popular analytical device is the use of Aristotle's dictum that the efficacy of speech-making can be measured in terms of the speaker's utilization of all the available means of persuasion. By following this procedure, critics may feel that they are absolving themselves of this particularly knotty situation of judging the speaker's ideas, and thus may feel safe in their scholarly work. This, up to a point, is a fallacy, as we shall see later on.

To be sure, there are other methods of assessment that the public address critic can use. Not all of these will thoroughly engage him, either as a man or a critic, although some will undoubtedly arouse his interest. Let us examine, in a large sense, some of the most popular critical and rhetorical approaches, and explain their implications as tools for judging the ideas and philosophy of a speaker. The critic should be aware, however, that even when he adopts one of the following methods, he is not completely objective for several reasons. The act of adoption, in itself, is a subjective act. How the critic uses the methodology is another.

If the critic of public address uses the results theory of the Sophists as his prime tool of assessment, he may draw some conclusions about the speaker's ideas. He could say that the speaker's views presented in his speech-making are good because they have been effective, because they have attained their ends. For example, the critic could say that Robert G. Ingersoll's philosophy, despite an outdated agnosticism, was good and useful according to the sophistic results theory. As a speaker, Ingersoll drew big crowds, was applauded at every turn, and, on another level, was elected to prominent political office. And since these were the results he desired and gained, he could and would be commended for the ideas and philosophy he held. This theory is popular in judging the orator as a whole, and not only his ideas. But it is perhaps not as valid, either objectively or subjectively, as many critics would like to believe. It is not valid because the criteria are not measuring what should be measured and evaluated. The validity of the ideas should be measured by rational, logical, and even intuitive hallmarks, rather than by such externals as their success in the market-place of a particular speaking situation. If the critic uses the results theory for measuring and evaluating the ideas of a speaker, he is to some extent denigrating his own responsibility as a critic of public address.[15]

Another rhetorical approach is the Platonist truth theory. This provides a set of instruments which probably have more reliability and validity for the assessment of ideas than the results theory of the Sophists. The Platonist approach to the criticism of a speaker's ideas is more philosophical than rhetorical. It may be that this is the reason why it is more valid.

Plato would advise that the ideas of a speaker are valid if they are philosophically sound rather than rhetorically acceptable. The latter hallmark, that of the Sophists, of course, was the basis of Plato's dispute with Gorgias. But the difficulty in assessing the ideas of a speaker by Plato's truth method is that the validity of the speaker's ideas can only be measured by Plato's philosophy. This could mean, as many critics of Plato have suggested, that the public address critic would need to be a philosopher rather than a rhetorician.

It is true that the public address critic using Plato's method would have to become acquainted with the total corpus of Plato's works. This would not necessarily mean that he would have to become a philosopher. The public address critic's first commitment, of course, is to rhetoric. In the process, he must attempt to master whatever instruments he needs for the job. If he subjectively chooses Plato's truth theory for his critical method, he cannot go about his task in a shallow way. He will need to comprehend Plato's basic theory: the theory of form and ideas. This Platonist approach indicates that what was important in life was not so much objects observable through the senses—the things we see, hear, and smell—but the ideas or form underlying them. To Plato the *idea* of a man which is static, unchanging, undying is more significant than the man himself who does change, deteriorates, and dies. Much of this development of Plato's views is found in his *The Phaedo*. The critic of public address should examine and understand this dialogue thoroughly.

But the critic, if he is to judge aright using Plato's truth theory, will also need to become conversant with other significant dialogues, as *The Gorgias, The Phaedrus, The Republic, The Statesman*. Only when the implications of these dialogues are related to the mainstream of Plato's ideas can the critic compare the orator's ideas and attitudes with those deemed important by Plato. Only then can the critic assess the ideas of a particular speaker and deem them useful, functional, acceptable, mediocre, wanting in value, or dangerous. There is a good deal of objectivity in this method. Even here, however, the interpretation of the orator's ideas via an interpretation of Plato's theory, and the weighing and judgment of these ideas are hardly completely objective. The process does have subjective aspects. Moreover, it has already been seen that the choice of Plato's theory, or any other, as the critical hallmark is an individual one, and therefore also subjective. After all, the critic can choose from many rhetorico-philosophico-politico-literary approaches for his judgment. The critic's choice reflects his attitude toward life and art, and is not only subjective, but also creative.

If the critic of public address is philosophically inclined, he can choose transcendental attitudes, or existential ones. If he is politically oriented, he can adopt one of that ever useful dichotomy: conservative or liberal criteria. He can also utilize radical stances, either of the far left or the far right. Then, too, he can select any political stance in between these two extremes. If he is theologically inclined, he has a large range of choices. Not only can he use the basic Christian ethic, but he can focus on the many facets of Christian doctrine such as Catholic, Episcopal, Lutheran, Methodist, Presbyterian, and others. But of course he is not limited to Christianity. He may also adopt Judaism, Zen, Buddhism, Hindu, Moslem, or any of the other non-Christian theologies extant today.

At first glance, it may seem that the critic of public address is getting far afield from his own narrow discipline when he moves into any one of these areas of philosophical, political, or religious thought for the evaluation of a speaker's ideas. In one sense he is, and he may be uncomfortable, feeling that scholars in the particular disciplines could do more effective work.

History, however, is full of scholars and critics who are neither parochial nor provincial; who rely on a full gamut of theoretical material for their critiques. It is in this broad arena that the most creatively useful work is usually done. Rhetorical critics have not yet journeyed into this realm, although their brothers-in-arms, the literary critics, have.

No more striking example is present than Vernon L. Parrington in his epoch-making volume, *Main Currents in American Thought*. Trained in literature, Parrington felt that the narrow boundaries of his own discipline needed to be transcended for effective evaluation. To that end his work used historical, literary, and rhetorical methods for its assessments. In addition, Parrington adopted a unique set of critical tools for measuring the ideological usefulness of the thinkers, writers, and speakers he studied. In his preface, he indicates that these criteria would be found in the various aspects of America's unique development. This development had come about, he thought, by the constant reciprocal action of the Hamiltonian-Jeffersonian philosophies of government. Here, it can be seen that the critic's hallmarks and eventual assessment produced insights never before given. Parrington is thus an exemplar of a creative critic of ideas who does not tarry on the well trod highways, but journeys into the realm, if not of the unknown, at least of the unforeseen.

Another example of critical creativity is Henry Steele Commager. Trained as a historian, Commager was intrigued with the Parrington method and with some variations made it his own in his useful critical volume, *The American Mind*. This is an interpretation of American thought and character since the 1880's. It is an evaluative work which concerns itself with such important and diverse aspects of American life as philosophy, literature, sociology, economics, history, politics, political theory, law, and architecture.

These are but two scholars and critics who were not fearful of moving toward horizons far removed from their own. Others in allied areas are Charles A. Beard, James Harvey Robinson, and Frederick Jackson Turner. They too gave unique achievements. There is no reason why the critic of public address cannot embark on a similar journey. In fact, some critics of public address must embark on such journeys if public address criticism is to be vivid, effective, and make significant contributions to our culture. If other literary scholars such as Lionel Trilling in *The Liberal Imagination* and Edmund Wilson in *To the Finland Station* and *Patriotic Gore* can utilize Freud and Marx, respectively, to assist them in formulating comprehensive literary and ideological judgments, there is no reason why the critic of public address cannot do the same. If he has the talent and the inclination, he can.

The use of Plato's truth theory can open up limitless philosophical horizons from which to view the world of ideas manifest in a speaker's thought. In a sense, the door to truth that was opened by Plato can also be opened by others. Each theorist and philosopher suggests that his theory for the evaluation of thought and concept is the true one. This omnipresent attitude only illustrates how dynamic truth can be for the critic. A number of such stances, following Plato, have been suggested. It is necessary to examine a third rhetorical viewpoint, in addition to the two already looked at—the Sophistic and the Platonist.

From Greece we journey to Rome to ascertain whether Quintilian, rhetorician and pedagogue, can offer us some tools for the assessment of ideas and philosophies. Quintilian's method, again perhaps oversimplified, has been dubbed the "Good Man" theory. Quintilian's views (which agreed with Cicero's in this regard) state that it is the good man speaking well who is adjudged to be the most effective. In the simplest terms, an individual is a great speaker if he is a good man. A good man to Quintilian is one who has the ingredients of intelligence, strength of character, and good will in his physical and psychological makeup. This may seem to have validity and reliability for the evaluation of a speaker as a whole, that is, of all his aspects of content and form; but what of its use in the realm of ideas? Can the "good man" theory be used in the evaluation and criticism of an orator's ideas and philosophy?

At first glance, perhaps, the assessment of a speaker's philosophical and social viewpoints through the utilization of the Quintilian method may not be easy to accomplish, or even practicable. Nevertheless, it may be of value if the attempt is made.

In actuality, of course, a person must manifest certain characteristics if he is to be dubbed a "good man." And only if he is a "good man" in the Quintilian sense will he be considered at least a good speaker, if not a great one. Now certainly part of a good man's character, intelligence, and perhaps even good will are the philosophical viewpoints he holds. Not that these views, promulgated in a speech, necessarily need to be accepted by all, as in a sophistic assessment of a person's ideas. But the critic using Quintilian's "good man" theory for the criticism of a person's philosophy perhaps should also consider factors other than *ethos*.

Here is another of those difficult reciprocal issues. To Quintilian and the Roman school of rhetoric a good man becomes one partially because of the views he holds. However, a man's total character can also enhance a man's ideas. The latter is probably more the case than the former.

More specifically, the success of many speakers stems a great deal more from their character and psyche than from their ideas. How else, from one point of view—that of political success, for instance—could we find such divergent but successful political figures as Woodrow Wilson and Calvin Coolidge, or Harry Truman and Dwight D. Eisenhower? Certainly the figures in each of these pairs were at odds ideologically. Thus, if one series of philosophical and social viewpoints were acceptable to the American people, then only the person holding those views, whether conservative or liberal, would be successful or great from the standpoint of speaking. We know, however, if we have examined the previous chapters dealing with historical background, and audience and occasion, that these factors are ever changing in society; and a man and his ideas may be accepted at one historical moment, but denied at another. This does not explain, however, the long political and speaking tenure of some prominent orators such as William Jennings Bryan or Henry Clay.

Part of the continued success of some politicos, as we have seen in the chapter delineating the biographical factors of the speaking situation, is the relative flexibility of their views. Henry Clay was extremely effective and gained results throughout his lifetime because he was not irrevocably committed to any given set of ideological values, unless we consider compromise such a value. This pragmatic compromiser continued in office for a lifetime and wielded more than a modicum of influence, with a set of very flexible ideas. Taking these factors into consideration still does not completely answer the problem of his oratorical and political success. The hidden ingredient is *ethos*—of character, intelligence, and good will—to use the well-known Roman hallmarks of rhetorical efficacy.

If all the above is true, can we scrutinize the ideas or philosophical viewpoints of a speaker in a critical way by using the Quintilian method? If so, the critical process will be one that is quite different from the two previously examined—that of the Sophists and Plato.

It has been ascertained that one of the significant components of a speaker's *ethos* is character. And character stems not merely from what a person says in public, but also from what he does. Each one supplements and complements the other. That is to say, character—or proof from character—probably comes from the reciprocal activity of what he says and what he does. The politician who has been in office attempts to build his image by bringing out in his public utterances the important actions in which he participated. These accomplishments, if they seem to fortify what a speaker stands for ideologically, enhance his image. Let us look at an example.

A liberal such as Hubert H. Humphrey, former senator from Minnesota, and now Vice-President, tried to implement his views by having a hand in passing appropriate legislation. As a senator, Humphrey's contributions to the passing of the act temporarily banning nuclear testing and civil rights legislation have enhanced his stature in the eyes of the liberal community, and perhaps even in the eyes of most of the people. Using Quintilian's criteria for evaluating a person's point of view, we could say then that Humphrey seems to be a good man because his ideas, implemented in action, have enhanced his character and good will and hence his *ethos*. These viewpoints, therefore, implemented in action, make him a good speaker.

If we attempt to evaluate a speaker's ideas by their subsequent effectiveness, we are really evaluating them not by any moral or ethical standards, but by results. And results are really the criteria of the Sophists, rather than those of Quintilian. What then, can we do? Must we say that Quintilian, Cicero, and the total corpus of Roman rhetorical theory offer no critical insights into a speaker?

In some respects, the good man in Quintilian's eyes has character dependent upon certain moral and ethical values. Primary among these is virtue. It must be remembered that the two dominant philosophies in the first century A.D. were those of Stoicism and Epicurianism. Stoicism was the philosophy, first articulated in 308 B.C. by Zeno, which believed that virtue was the highest good. The Epicurians looked to the good life, and refused to be perturbed by any physical or religious doctrines which would impose duties upon them and thus hinder their freedom of pure enjoyment. This manifestly was not the Quintilian view.

The Stoics considered virtue alone as the sole good. The virtuous man was one who had attained happiness through knowledge. Knowledge was obtained through disciplining one's self. Socrates is an example. The Roman seeking happiness finds it in himself. He is independent to a great extent of the external world. He has succeeded in overcoming it by mastering himself, his passions, and his emotions. No matter what happened to him, he could retain virtue. He could be poor, but he could be virtuous;

he could be thrown into prison, but he could still have virtue. He could be forced to suffer all sorts of corporal punishments, but his virtue could not be taken away from him. He could even be punished by death, but could still retain the one good, virtue. In other words, true virtue could never be taken away from him, if he desired to retain it. This Stoic ideal was influential in molding Quintilian's philosophy of life and hence his theory of rhetoric. One can readily see that moral and ethical considerations went into Quintilian's theory.

Thus, the primary assessment that we can give the speaker's ideas, if we use the Quintilian hallmarks, is based on moral considerations. Quintilian as a rhetorician can assist us by suggesting that the utilization of ethical criteria is most significant in criticizing a man's ideological viewpoints.

We will then be using Quintilian as a moralist. Quintilian can be so interpreted when we say that a man's character must have integrity, power of will, stick-to-itiveness, and the other moral virtues. In attempting to assess a speaker's ideas, the critic will not attempt to criticize them in their pure form only, that is, in a form unrelated to the individual. He will see whether the speaker holds his views through genuine commitment or for other reasons. Politicians have made reputations and have been considered good speakers often because of this sole good of commitment to a cause. Robert A. Taft, late senator from Ohio, immediately comes to mind as an example. People who did not necessarily agree with Taft's conservative views admired him as a man, and hence as a speaker, because of this kind of honest commitment to the conservative ideal. Of course, there were other facets in Taft's character that implemented this view, but this kind of integrity was justifiably a useful component in Taft's *ethos*, and thus in his speaking power. Individuals who evaluated Taft in this manner and by these standards were using the Quintilian theory in their assessments.

The critic, influenced by Quintilian, might see whether the person's ideas are held primarily because of expediency. If a speaker says one thing, constantly propounding a specific philosophical or social view, for instance, but often acts in another fashion, he lacks integrity and thus *ethos*. He would not be a good man, and therefore, not a good speaker.

The reverse would also be true. One kind of honesty is shown by practicing what one preaches; telling the truth is another. Both make a good man, and an effective speaker.

But these assessments are still tangential to the main issue. What of the ideas themselves that the speaker propounds? What of the invention of his speeches? How can the critic say whether the views of the speaker are good, useful, correct?

Here, too, the moral ingredient manifests itself. Here probably Quintilian would be closer to Plato than to the Sophists. The dictator who denied freedom of speech, who believed in a society that did not disseminate equal justice for all, who held men in subservience, or inculcated a reign of terror, obviously would not be a good man, and hence not a good speaker. Adolf Hitler would be such an orator despite his vaunted effectiveness and the results of his speechmaking. The critic of public address who utilizes the Quintilian criteria for criticizing the ideas of a speaker would use moral and ethical judgments in his analysis and assessment.

Quintilian, writing in Rome many centuries ago, would not indicate moral criteria which would be completely acceptable in America today. A critic attempting to evaluate ideas and philosophies of a speaker today would probably best emulate the Quintilian ethic, if he were to use moral and ethical value judgments. Thus, his criticism, stemming from the Roman rhetorical theorist, is not only rhetorical but probably ethical and social as well. These criteria have their value in the arsenal of the public address critic.

But what of the fourth great classical rhetorical theorist, Aristotle? Can he be of any assistance to the critic of public address in the evaluation of ideas and philosophical viewpoints of an individual? Where should we look in Aristotle to find aid in evaluating ideas?

Aristotle's *Rhetoric*, as such, probably is not as helpful

in this regard as his other works. The *Rhetoric* is sub-divided into three main parts: the speaker, the audience, and the speech. The first part, that dealing with the speaker, perhaps may be described as mainly logical and political; the second, with its emphasis on the audience, is primarily ethical or psychological; the third, in which the speech itself is the focus, is mainly literary or stylistic. The *Rhetoric*, therefore, is more concerned with indicating the proper practice of a speaker than it is with giving the critic tools for assessment. Benchmarks for criticism, to be sure, can be gleaned from Aristotle's theory, as they can from the theory of almost every rhetorical theorist.

Aristotle's celebrated dicta—that rhetoric is the counterpart of dialectic and the utilization of all the available means of persuasion—leave little room for the practice of ideological criticism. The first statement, while it does not completely negate the use of rhetoric as the *discovery* of truth, does suggest that rhetoric's role is the *energizing* of the truth already discovered via dialectic or through other means. It does not concern itself with ideas or the validity of a person's political or social philosophy. The second statement suggests a functional relationship among speaker, audience, occasion, and the times. It gives little in the way of standards by which ideas are to be judged.

Most rhetorical critics today are enamored with the Aristotelian formulations and use them in their own studies. This may be the reason why there is so little effective evaluative criticism of public address by rhetorical critics. There is an abundance of descriptive studies. Even of analytical works there is a goodly number. The critic following the *Rhetoric* is concerned primarily with the speaker's use of the means available to him. If the speaker used most of the means available, then he is usually thought of as quite effective; if he did not, then he is usually judged as less than effective. The ideas available to the speaker can also be evaluated, but they seldom are. In the rare cases where this kind of assessment has been made, this is still not an evaluation of the ideas themselves.

If the *Rhetoric* does not indicate standards for judging

the ideologies held by a speaker, other of Aristotle's works do accomplish that aim. Probably the most useful are the *Ethics* and the *Politics*. These two works extend the material in the *Rhetoric*, especially the material dealing with the political and ethical factors. Whereas in the *Rhetoric* politics and ethics are dealt with on the objective level, in the *Politics* and the *Ethics* Aristotle sets up hallmarks by which ideas can actually be judged. These standards can be useful if the public address critic accepts the Aristotelian dicta on the good society and the good man. The Aristotelian "golden mean," for example, is one such criterion. It can be a useful evaluative instrument in the judgment of ideas. This is one relatively easy method that the critic can follow in the criticism of ideas of a speaker. The other method, coming from Aristotle and available to the critic, is more difficult, but perhaps ultimately more rewarding. It is the so-called inductive method.

Aristotle uses the inductive method in most of his writings. The *Politics* and the *Ethics* are inductive in character as are the *Rhetoric* and the *Poetics*. The conclusions in these works do not come so much from the intuitive or speculative faculties of the master Greek as they emanate from his rational observations of society. This does not make them less useful. In fact, what is so valuable in the *Ethics* and the *Politics* is not so much the Aristotelian "golden mean" in the former, or Aristotle's celebration of the good society in the latter. It is another quality that is also valuable in his *Rhetoric* and *Poetics*. This quality is the inductive method used rather than any specific injunctions given in his works. It is unfortunate for rhetorical criticism that so few critics have recognized this inductive factor and subsequently used it in their own critiques. Yet it is understandable because the utilization of the inductive process in criticism is not easy. And critics, like most human beings, do not look for the most difficult road to follow.

A close study by the public address critic of Aristotle's work would suggest a methodology for discovering standards useful in ideological judgment. The critic following this procedure then, would not outline a series of measuring devices coming from the *Ethics* and *Politics* (as most rhetorical and literary critics have done from the *Rhetoric* and *Poetics*). Rather he would seek those criteria contained in the works of Aristotle related to the total cultural context in which he lived. The critic would then be following the Aristotelian process because the great Greek philosopher drew his conclusions from his own socio-cultural milieu.

Once this relation of classic ideas to classic times is discovered and made clear, the critic of public address can follow a similar procedure in unearthing and setting up standards for contemporary ideological judgment. These would be arrived at by the allied process of relating contemporary ideas and viewpoints to contemporary culture. These standards, modified by the times and social situation, would comprise a series of measuring tools that the contemporary critic could use for his own assessments of contemporary orators.

It is here that the public address critic is on fallow ground. Here he can make effective contributions via his criticism. Of course, the critic must be aware that in the process of discovering his unique critical tools for assessing ideological viewpoints, he has himself followed a process which used description, analysis, and criticism. This large task can be consummated for its eventual use in criticism, and for its own intrinsic value.

During this process of discovery, the critic must also be aware that his own fallibility is a factor in the inductive unearthing of the critical laws which he will follow. Finally, he must realize that this is a dynamic process and is therefore not stable, absolute, or universal, but rather, constantly changing. Once the critic has found the standards for judging ideas of a certain orator at a certain juncture of history, he can probably apply them only to other speakers during the same period and within a similar cultural context. He usually could not utilize the same criteria for speakers of a generation later. It would be a gross critical error, for instance, to apply ideological hallmarks of the 1890's to those of the 1920's.

Yet we often apply critical ideological benchmarks from the 18th century to those of our own times, and we expect these to have lasting reliability and value.

If the critic has done the above, he also has made value judgments about ideas and philosophies which he would use in assessing speakers' viewpoints. In one way, this is close to the moral judgments of Quintilian, although arrived at through the inductive process. In another way, however, this is the most creative kind of evaluation. Here the critic is searching for truth, and in writing criticism, he also attempts to disseminate his own vision of the truth. In the realm of rhetoric and society, he can attempt to answer questions, even if somewhat generally. He may try to answer questions such as the following: How theoretically useful, effective, and true are the ideas? How operationally valid and reliable are the ideas?

This means that the critic has difficulty in finding criteria and criticizing ideologies of a speaker. The critic's work is further complicated by the problem of synthesis. Here the difficulty lies in welding description, analysis, interpretation, and evaluation into a comprehensive and effective whole. Nevertheless, the job can be done.

Arthur M. Schlesinger, Jr., shows one example in *The Politics of Upheaval,* in his evaluation of the economic ideas in the speaking of the prominent radio priest of the 1930's, Father Charles E. Coughlan. It will be noted in the following excerpt that the assessment occurs within the framework of a particular cultural context. About Coughlan, Schlesinger writes:

> He detested capitalism for its callousness, its individualism, its atheism; most of all, for its domination by bankers, and especially by international bankers. . . . These "modern Shylocks" had caused depression; now, in their greed for profit, they were preventing recovery. Bankers gained their profits by making money scarce; this artificial shortage of money was the bottleneck which constricted the flow of goods from the factories and farms to the people. Without means of payment, "capitalism could not go on any more than a human being equipped for the operation of breathing air could go on when submerged in the waters of the

ocean." Given the money shortage, "the only two ways out are revaluation of our gold ounce, or repudiation of our debts. One way is Christianity. The other way is Bolshevism."

Beginning in 1932, Coughlan began to press his demands for the Christian solution. His orations now bristled with economic statistics and syllogisms. Part of this air of authority came from two New York businessmen, George LeBlanc, a banker, and Robert M. Harriss, a cotton broker, both convinced isolationists. Coughlan also used papers on economic questions written to his order by students at the Brookings Institution. The revaluation of gold was only the first step in a sound—i.e., inflationary—monetary program. Next, he said, must come the remonetization of silver, both to broaden the base of the currency and to enable the Orient to regain its purchasing power. Here again the international bankers, who had driven silver out of circulation many years before, were the villains. Silver, Coughlan warned sententiously, "has a value and always will, long after the slave standard of the Rothschilds will have been forgotten." And if the people were to recapture control over money, Coughlan believed, the government must nationalize the banks, "creating a nationally-owned banking system as sound as our army and as honest as our post office." This demand was the heart of Coughlan's program.

This program was by no means irrelevant. Coughlan was, of course, more correct than the orthodox economists of 1932 in his preference for inflation over deflation. His plea for monetary management was defensible. Certainly these were fairly basic issues. But his economics were nonetheless rudimentary, specious, and incoherent. He gave indiscriminate support to nearly every available monetary nostrum without regard to logic or consistency. A bill drawn up to embody his ideas and introduced by Gerald Nye in the Senate and Martin Sweeney in the House was abysmally vague. For Coughlan economics was a minor branch of rhetoric.[16]

The American Mind by Henry Steele Commager follows to some extent the Parrington method of evaluation. While definite in statement, it is yet more subtle than the comments of Schlesinger. However, when one reads Commager's assessment of a person's philosophy, one can sense immediately the approving note of accolade, or the disapproving one of condemnation. One can readily discern the former in the following excerpt about William Jennings Bryan. Commager in his evaluation states:

> William Jennings Bryan was not a political philosopher, and many would deny his title to statesmanship. Yet his political creed was born of an instinctive understanding of the meaning of American history, and he pioneered in the advocacy of more and more important legislation than any other politician of his generation. The most representative American of his time, he represented what was, on the whole, soundest and most wholesome in the American character. His democracy was intuitive but none the less rationalized for that; his moral earnestness grew out of religious convictions; his economic radicalism was a product of experience familiar enough to those born and raised along the Middle Border. He spoke for the God-fearing, Protestant, evangelical America, for the rural America that was giving way to the urban, for the South and the West whose resources were being exploited to profit the East, for the homespun, egalitarian America dismayed at the emergence of social classes and exotic standards, and he spoke with the tongue of angels. Less sophisticated than Theodore Roosevelt, less profound than Wilson, not so hardheaded as La Follette, he was neither the simpleton nor the demagogue that his critics pictured and that a later generation, misled by Dayton and Coral Gables, imagined. Without any profound grasp of economics, he knew as much about the tariff or the money question as most contemporary politicians—and rather more than Mark Hanna or the silver-plated McKinley—and as his instincts were sound he managed to penetrate to the nature, though not to the solution, of the economic problems that harassed his followers. Lacking in critical acumen, he had nevertheless a firm grasp on political and economic realities, and, though he clothed all his arguments in trailing clouds of rhetoric, the arguments themselves were logical enough. He was the first major figure to give articulate expression to the rumblings of discontent that were sweeping the nation, the first to understand that the problems of politics were primarily economic, the first to formulate a broad program designed to translate the hopes of the nineteenth-century democracy into policies relevant to the practical needs of the twentieth. The most astute politician of his day, he never compromised his integrity; the most ambitious, he never sacrificed principle to ambition; three times rejected

by the American people, he never wavered in his faith in their virtue or in the essential soundness of their judgment, and he gloried in the name, "The Great Commoner." He had an understanding of the psychology of his own kind that has never been surpassed and inspired such devotion in them as few other American statesmen have been able to command.

Of the new forces transforming American political thought—evolution, pragmatism, economics, and psychology —he was wanting in comprehension of only the second. He knew, none better, that the Constitution had to be adjusted to the needs of a twentieth-century society, and for two decades he led the fight on laissez-faire; all his political campaigns were economic—though it was an economics curiously blended with morals; his understanding of popular psychology was shrewd and enlightened. But, unlike his contemporaries, La Follette, Theodore Roosevelt, and Wilson, he was wholly lacking in the scientific habit of mind, and for the expert he had only distrust—a distrust which was generously reciprocated. He is the connecting link between the nineteenth and twentieth centuries, embodying the best of the American character that was rapidly becoming archaic, anticipating the political program designed to adjust that character to the complex demands of the new day. The people whose battles he so gallantly fought have all but forgotten him; the causes he championed were to be vindicated under new leaders; his reputation has been buried among the ruins of his own triumphs.[17]

Commager's cogent statement is an assessment of Bryan's views—one can immediately discern that Commager considers them good and useful for the time, if not exemplary—as well as an important analysis tying the ideas to the man. As such, it is also a pithy evaluation of Bryan's total image and personality, since ideas and philosophies play a distinct role in the ethical appeal of an individual.

The process of selecting standards by which to judge the efficacy and value of the philosophies of individuals is a difficult one. Henry Alonzo Myers, however, in *Are Men Equal?* is equal to the task. In a critique of William Graham Sumner, the Social Darwinist whose philosophy was to a great extent anti-democratic and anti-equalitarian, Myers juxtaposes the egalitarian concept. In the process, he shows how and why the concept of equality can be a moral and functional criterion. Myers says:

> When men seek a universal standard to replace the divisive moral codes which serve the selfish interests of individuals and factions, they necessarily turn to the axiom of equality. The Sermon on the Mount, high point in the unfolding Jewish-Christian tradition of the fatherhood of God and the brotherhood of man, centers on the golden rule: "Therefore all things whatsoever ye would that men should do to you, do ye even so to them: for this is the law and the prophets." Kant's dream of universal peace had a down-to-earth foundation in his version of the moral law: "we should so act as to treat humanity in ourselves and others in every case as an end, never as a means only." Jeremy Bentham's inquiry into the possibility of utmost happiness for all inspired his famous dictum: "Everybody to count for one, nobody for more than one." His disciple, John Stuart Mill, maintained that Bentham's utilitarianism is identical in spirit with the golden rule. He was right. Every ethical system which aims at human welfare takes equality as its starting point. How, then, can men ever be proved unequal in worth by an ethical standard?
>
> Since ethical standards are always burdensome, many Americans were willing to ease their democratic consciences under the new standard of industrial virtue. When the proposition of equality checked their appetites for power, they discovered its "inherent absurdity"; when government by the people set limits to their economic freedom, they questioned the expediency of Lincoln's "jingle." In their fight to prevent democratic changes in the status quo, they welcomed nature as an ally, and rejoiced in the "science" which proves that free competition is justly founded on natural law and that the ability to acquire capital is the highest form of righteousness. They were on top economically and socially: and they were confident that they were strong enough to stay on top, provided the underdogs were not permitted to change the rules of the game.[18]

This brief analysis in depth of a significant idea from both a positive and negative view, indicates what is needed to discover the functional value of the criteria for judging the views of individuals.

Finally, the significant relationship of philosophies to men and social and cultural trends is best explained in Crane Brinton's *The Shaping of the Modern Mind*. This is the concluding half of Brinton's very useful study of the history of Western thought, *Ideas and Men*. About the logical positivists and their function within the movement of anti-intellectualism, Brinton has this to say:

> Very briefly, logical positivism asserts that the only valid kind of knowledge is cumulative knowledge, the kind one finds in natural science. For this kind of knowledge there exists a process, the process gradually worked out in Western culture by our scientists, through which one can test the truth of any statement that is claimed to be knowledge. In Bridgman's term, you can perform an operation on the statement—sometimes a long and difficult operation involving laboratory and field research, much mathematics and hard logical thinking—but an operation that will enable you to test the truth or falsity of the statement.[19]

After this introduction, Brinton begins the more significant and elaborate process of analysis and the subtle but distinct procedure of evaluation and criticism.

> The logical positivist tends to regard all traditional philosophic thinking, the kind involved in fields like metaphysics, ethics, political theory, even most epistemology and of course pure Aristotelian logic, as a complete waste of time; the favorite figure of speech compares the traditional philosopher with the squirrel in his treadmill cage.
> The logical positivists are themselves most abstract thinkers, whose positive interest is chiefly the modern extension of the mathematician's way of going at things that is called symbolic logic. Some of the more innocent of them hoped that once they had worked out symbolic logic to perfection all communications in symbolic logic would be perfectly understandable by all human beings, who would thenceforth never quarrel, since they would never suffer from ignorance and misunderstanding. But mostly the logical positivists simply pushed aside these questions of moral and aesthetic standards (value-judgments) as to them "meaningless." They did not really believe that just because no scientific answer to these questions could be found there were in fact as many answers as there were

human beings on earth. They were not, in their practice, moral cynics or nihilists. They simply took values as not to be thought about profitably, a point of view annoying to those brought up in prevailing Western traditions, which have tended to hold that some judgments about morals and aesthetics are truer, or at least make more sense, than others.

Yet since from its more innocent to its more sophisticated forms anti-intellectualism emphasizes the immense role of the irrational in men's lives, there is a constant temptation of the anti-intellectualist to see only the clear-cut triumph of the objective thinking we call natural science. Heir to the long Western tradition of tough-mindedness, he is afraid of the kind of thinking Newman defended as the work of the illative sense. He sees that *all* sane men of sufficient education can be convinced of the truth of certain propositions in physics; he sees that *all* sane men of sufficient education simply cannot be convinced of any propositions in English literature—beyond simple statements of fact, such as that William Shakespeare wrote a play called *Romeo and Juliet*. And, at that, there are those who maintain that Francis Bacon wrote the play! Yet, of course the position that on any statement save simple statements of verifiable fact and statements of scientifically established uniformities one man's opinion is just as good as another's, the position that, as Bentham once declared, "pushpin is as good as poetry," is one that most men—even anti-intellectuals—find displeasing.[20]

Brinton concludes the critique by indicating the significance of his idea in a penetrating paragraph that differentiates the utility of value-judgments from the utility of factual statements held by the logical positivists. He writes:

One way out for them we have seen already suggested by Machiavelli and Nietzsche: The truth of these value-judgments may not be rationally establishable, but their importance in the social life of a given culture *can* be established. A society that believes in the efficacy of certain religious rites wholly incapable of scientific justification may yet gain strength from such belief. Pareto cites as an example a Greek crew in ancient times sacrificing to Poseidon, god of the sea, before they set sail on a dangerous voyage; we today should be willing to accept regarding Poseidon the logical positivist's verdict that there is no possible proof of his existence; yet, says Pareto, it is clear that if under the influence of the belief that they had put themselves right with Poseidon the crew rowed more heartily, maintained better discipline, stuck together better under pressure of danger, then clearly belief in Poseidon was useful to them, and in a sense true.[21]

Numerous examples from critics other than rhetoricians might be pertinent as evaluations of significant ideas and views of thinkers, writers, and speakers. Morton White's *Social Thought in America*[22] makes interesting reading for anyone intrigued with the decline of what White calls formalism. His dissections of John Dewey, James Harvey Robinson, Charles A. Beard, and Justice Oliver W. Holmes are penetrating and insightful, although quite different from the assessments of the same men by Henry Steele Commager in *The American Mind.*

The interpretation and criticism of the ideas of American speakers can be approached from many different points of view. Such theories as those of the general semanticists, the empiricists, the romanticists, or the humanists, although not explored in the preceding pages, can obviously prove fruitful. For no one method or theory of ideological criticism is absolutely correct. Thus, there is no attempt here to project a view of the world which can be accepted and utilized by *all* critics of public address. Instead, a few possibilities from the classical rhetorical theorists have been presented. The examples, however, have come from other genres, those of history, philosophy, and social thought. These two groups of suggestions should open the way to further research. It is up to the critic himself to select from among the many viewpoints available to him those from which he can operate most efficaciously within the critical dimension.

The critic should be aware of the fallibility of his own judgments and of his criteria as well. Not all criteria for criticism have equal value. This does not mean, however, that he should emulate that interesting character in Albert Camus' striking novella, *The Plague.* This individual could not write beyond the first paragraph of his epic because he was unhappy with what he had stated there, and how he had stated it. One of the implications is that this character lacked commitment, and, therefore, could not function effectively. The public address critic should not fall into the same trap. If he is to make valuable contributions to rhetoric and to society, he must engage himself; he must select the criteria in which he thoroughly believes; and once committed, he must do the best he can in his own work. He will not know whether he is right or wrong. He must let posterity decide that for him.

QUESTIONS AND PROJECTS

1. In what way does Arthur M. Schlesinger, Jr., in the three-volume work entitled *The Age of Roosevelt* criticize the ideas of such men as Herbert Hoover, Huey Long, Wendell Willkie?

2. Select a book containing a series of essays on prominent men, such as Edmund Wilson's *Patriotic Gore*, and see if if you can discern what standards for ideological criticism the author uses.

3. Write a short paper indicating what the main problems are in the criticism of ideas and philosophies.

4. What are the contributions that a public address critic can make to social criticism?

5. What are some of the reasons you would use in a paper defending the right of the public address critic to criticize and evaluate ideas?

6. Write a short paper indicating the reasons against the public address critic journeying into the realm of ideological assessment.

7. Select a prominent speaker of the twentieth century and write a short paper criticizing the social views that he held.

8. Write a series of criteria by which you would assess the social views of a speaker. Do the same for a speaker's religious views.

9. In a short essay justify the use of Cicero's standards for judging the effectiveness of an orator's views.

NOTES

1. Anthony Hillbruner, "Inequality, The Great Chain of Being and Ante-Bellum Southern Oratory," *Southern Speech Journal*, XXV, 3 (Spring, 1960), 179.

2. Arthur O. Lovejoy, *The Great Chain of Being* (Cambridge: Harvard University Press, 1936), p. 50.

3. Aristotle, *Metaphysics* X, 1069a5, quoted in *ibid*, p. 55.

4. *Ibid.*, p. 58.

5. Aristotle, *De Anima*, quoted in *ibid.*, pp. 58–59.

6. Lovejoy, *ibid.*, p. 59.

7. Hillbruner, *op. cit.*, p. 174.

8. Lovejoy, *op. cit.*, p. 205.

9. Hillbruner, *op cit.*, p. 175.

10. *Ibid.*, p. 182.

11. Henry Cleveland, *Alexander H. Stephens in Public and Private, With Letters and Speeches During and Since the War* (Philadelphia: National Publishing Co., 1866), p. 650. Italics mine.

12. Hillbruner, *op. cit.*, p. 183.

13. *Ibid*.

14. *Ibid.*, p. 184

15. The term public address critic is used in these pages more often than rhetorical critic or speech critic (although the latter two are utilized for the sake of stylistic variety) because of the implication or connotation of these terms. Rhetorical, or speech, criticism connotes the utilization of rhetorical criteria exclusively. Public address criticism, within the context of this work, suggests a good deal more. The perusal of the preceding and succeeding pages should indicate what that much more is. Suffice it to say at this point, that public address criticism attempts to use rhetorical *and* social hallmarks. Moreover, this should be manifest especially in the assessment of ideas by the critic; although it is hoped that this book should indicate the usefulness of these varied benchmarks for other aspects of the total public address situation. Probably what it is hoped that this volume will do is to indicate a desire for, and a utilization of, an inductive approach in the criticism. And this approach, as is well known, suggests that the tools for the criticism should be forged from the material to be assessed itself. Only then can they be used in a particular situation.

16. Arthur M. Schlesinger, Jr., *The Politics of Upheaval* (Boston: Houghton, Mifflin, 1960), pp. 19–20.
17. Henry Steele Commager, *The American Mind* (New Haven: Yale University Press, 1950), pp. 346–347.
18. Henry Alonzo Myers, *Are Men Equal?* (copyright, 1945, by Henry Alonzo Myers; first published, G. P. Putnam's Sons, 1945; reissued, Cornell University Press, 1955), pp. 142–143.
19. Crane Brinton, *The Shaping of the Modern Mind* (New York: New American Library, 1950), p. 234.
20. *Ibid.*, pp. 234–235.
21. *Ibid.*, p. 235.
22. Morton White, *Social Thought in America* (Boston: Beacon Press, 1957).

SELECTED BIBLIOGRAPHY

Brinton, Crane, *The Shaping of the Modern Mind,* New York: New American Library, 1950.

Commager, Henry Steele, *The American Mind,* New Haven: Yale University Press, 1950.

Hillbruner, Anthony, "Criticism as Persuasion," *Southern Speech Journal,* XXVIII, 4 (Summer, 1963), 260–267.

———, "Plato and Korzybski: Two Views of Truth in Rhetorical Theory," *Southern Speech Journal,* XXIV, 4 (Summer, 1959), 185–196.

Muller, Herbert J., *Freedom in the Ancient World,* New York: Harper & Row, 1961.

———, *The Uses of the Past,* New York: Oxford University Press, 1952.

Myers, Henry Alonzo, *Are Men Equal?,* Ithaca, New York: Cornell University Press, 1955.

Nilson, Thomas R., "Interpretative Function of the Critic," *Western Speech,* XXI, 2 (Spring, 1957), 70–76.

Parrington, Vernon L., *Main Currents in American Thought,* New York: Harcourt, Brace, 1930, Vol. I, "Introduction."

White, Morton, *Social Thought in America,* Boston: Beacon Press, 1957.

Wilson, Edmund, *Patriotic Gore,* New York: Oxford University Press, 1962.

7 Description
and Analysis of
Speechmaking

We come now to what many a student has long been
waiting for, namely, the speech itself. Everything up to
this point has been merely prelude, he might say, to the
criticism of the speeches themselves. He would be correct,
but only up to a point. For it is true that if the student
masters the preceding material, he will be prepared for
the criticism ahead. It is also true, however, that a rhetorical critic can devote his scholarly life to one or another
aspect of criticism discussed in the previous chapters and
make a unique and useful contribution to criticism, to
society, and to knowledge. Perhaps more rhetorical critics
should do so. Certainly the literature of speech criticism
would be enriched by these studies.

Nevertheless, most student critics are justifiably eager
to get to the speech or speeches. But even here some
preliminary materials are necessary. This chapter will be
devoted to the discovery and description of what was
said in a specific speech or a series of speeches, and how
it was said. This is rhetorical description and analysis.

Description and analysis are actually two different but
closely related procedures.

Descriptive materials are those relatively simple elu-
cidations of the speech's content and form. That is to say,
the critic tries to understand what the speaker said and
how he said it. Usually this is not too difficult. Thus, he
will first explain, to himself if not to his reading audience,
exactly what the speaker's message was. This is the stage
of paraphrase. The critic needs to know the speech so

well that he can give any part of it in his own words. Then, the critic will look to formal elements other than the invention: the canons of arrangement, style, delivery, and memory or the oral command of these materials. The proofs used and the descriptive material may also shed light on the audience and the occasion.

While some of this work may seem to be very elementary research in rhetorical scholarship, not all of it is so simple. And some description encroaches upon analysis. For as soon as you break a speech into its salient aspects—introduction, thesis, body, and conclusion—you are more in the realm of analysis than description. This is the main reason that the two procedures of description and analysis are considered in the same chapter. They are inextricably tied together. Also, the process of paraphrase, especially of a somewhat esoteric lecture by Reinhold Niebuhr or Paul Tillich, for instance, impinges upon the analytical or even the interpretative procedure. While the central theme of a speech may not be too difficult to ascertain, the development of that theme can be. For full comprehension, this kind of descriptive paraphrasing must be accomplished well.

This naturally leads to the second procedure—that of analysis. While description with its analogues of analysis and even interpretation tries to stay on the purely objective level by indicating the main factors in the speech, the analysis usually goes deeper by attempting to answer the question of how the speaker availed himself of particular materials. Thus, the inferential reasoning enters the picture, supplying its own useful discernments. And inferences are not the same for every individual, student, or critic. This factor is present in addition to the factual data, and must be dealt with perceptively.

Profitable studies of the various salient and minor aspects of rhetoric can be written not only for their understanding of the speaker as a whole but also for their intrinsic value. For example, what has been called derisively computer research—the counting of the figures of speech used in an address, the analogies, the number of long and short sentences, or the use of the pronoun "I"—has gone out of fashion in both literary and rhetorical study. Nonetheless, if any of these can be related in some effective fashion to speaker, occasion, or time, it may have intrinsic merit. They should not be completely scorned. Almost anything that is done in rhetorical description or analysis that sheds some light on the speaking process can be useful as criticism in the largest sense.

The "what" of description and the "how" of analysis are prime tools for the public address critic. Facility in explication of the factual materials and the effective use of analysis will go far to prepare the writer for the interpretation and the assessment which is to be made later. It is a valid assertion that if these two steps are dealt with cursorily, then what will follow as interpretation and assessment will not be very reliable. For example, the question of how exemplary organization in a speech accomplished a certain purpose, is highly significant and should be composed and developed with careful attention to the analytical factors.

In using the above process, the public address critic breaks down his material into its component parts. Insofar as arrangement is concerned, the critic should try to give enough details to illustrate how arrangement is most efficaciously used to develop and support the orator's views. It is not enough merely to say that the organizational format is of a certain well-known type; that it follows a problem-solving sequence; that it is topical in arrangement; that it is primarily chronological; or that it attempts an inductive or implicative approach. The critic needs to be specific to prove his case, and to give penetrating insights into the speech and the particular speaking situation. He needs to show how a specific pattern of idea development detracted from the speaker's effectiveness, had little relevance for it, or was the best possible format the speaker could have used—to cite three simple analytical possibilities. Many variations and modifications on these three themes are possible. Thus, a process of inference and reasoning comes from the descriptive factual data. It is in this fashion that analysis sets the stage for later evaluation.

The public address critic will be aware that this procedure can be used in a single speech or in a series of

speeches, such as the Lincoln-Douglas debates, or else-
where. A descriptive and analytical study could be made
of the major themes of a prominent orator's addresses
during a certain period. Or the total oratorical output of
a speaker's career could be analyzed. The latter is a large
scale order that would take a great deal of time and could
even be a proper subject for a dissertation or a full size
book, rather than an article or a monograph.

To be sure, a study of this analytical type can also be
made of any major or minor formal elements of speechmaking. An example might be a study of style in the speaking of John F. Kennedy, encompassing the stylistic development of early speeches compared with that of later
ones. Also, since Kennedy's earliest ambition was to be
a journalist, and since he did some serious writing,
(*Profiles in Courage* and *Why England Slept*), there is
opportunity for a comparative study of his style in his
writings and speeches. Or it could be a large scale in-
vestigation of the changes in Kennedy's style from his
earliest public utterances to his last ones. The same sort
of scrutiny could be made on the descriptive and analytical level of any other formal elements. The logical proofs
used in the Nixon-Kennedy debates of 1960, or the use of
emotional or ethical appeals in the debates, are two elements that are evocative and might provide useful discernments concerning the two main antagonists for the
Presidency in that fateful campaign.

In the description and analysis of delivery and memory
of an orator, the critic is on more tentative ground. In the
formal elements mentioned earlier, those of arrangement
and style, for example, the critic can trust his own knowledge and discernment. He can bring his own creative
abilities, his own scholarly-aesthetic insights to the data
and analysis of the proofs. But in the description and
analysis of the formal aspect of presentation, he is highly
dependent on other observers and critics. He must use
secondary sources much of the time. And while these can
be very useful, often there is a divergency of views, even
among witnesses to the speaking of prominent figures.

Individuals in audiences often hear only what they
want to hear, and only in the way they want to hear it.

Furthermore, many persons are unlearned and unsophisticated in discerning the finer nuances of the delivery of a particular speaker. Then, too, friends and foes have different views of an orator's delivery. This fact is seen in the divergency of opinions on the oral presentation of Abraham Lincoln. During the series of debates with Douglas in Illinois in 1858, the Democratic press in the state dealt harshly not only with Lincoln's ideas but with his presentation of them as well. The Republican newspapers like the *Chicago Tribune* lauded the prairie lawyer's invention and delivery. Even such a reputed poor speaker —from the standpoint of delivery—as Thomas Jefferson has had his defenders among those who heard him. His "First Inaugural Address," for instance, had received accolades for its quiet confident tone and firm manner of delivery, as well as its significant theme. One can readily see what is meant by the fallibility of the accounts of actual auditors to the speechmaking, especially if these auditors are laymen. However, even unearthing a divergency of opinion about such a canon as delivery can aid the critic in his final judgment.

The analysis of another neglected aspect of speechmaking, that of memory—the complete grasp and command of the materials of a speech—considered by some rhetoricians as a lost canon, is also valuable in itself. It also has other virtues. It can be an aid in seeing into the inner recesses of the speaker's character.

Its intrinsic value lies in illustrating methods of preparation, as well as delivery. It is valuable in providing insights into character in several ways. Certainly whether a speaker uses a manuscript, memorizes the speech verbatim, or speaks from notes tells us something about him. It tells us something about the power of his memory, and it indicates his cursory or complete involvement in his material and in his ideas. The degree of glibness, garrulousness, or loquaciousness illustrates the varying extent of an individual's talkativeness. These analytical conclusions, in turn, show certain important factors of the speaker's psyche, which again, in turn, relate to his speaking prowess.

A contemporary speaker and politician, Hubert Horatio

Humphrey, exemplifies the value of this aspect of speech-making for the individual and, hence, for the critic of public address. The former Minnesota Senator and now Vice-President of the United States has made his reputation by his command of both domestic and foreign governmental policy. This grasp of the material and its subsequent effectiveness for formal speechmaking and informal speaking at press conferences has had a great deal to do with Humphrey's ever more successful forays into politics. It gives us useful discernments and helpful grounds for an evaluation of the ebullient personality of Hubert Horatio Humphrey.

Another specific aim of the description and analysis of an individual's speaking is to compare and contrast either content or form in the different speeches. Still another aim would be to compare, contrast, and interrelate the orator's spoken and written speeches on levels other than the stylistic. This procedure is not always fruitful, but some interesting contrasts can be discovered between the statements presented in a written fashion and off-the-cuff utterances, particularly in a heated political campaign. Harry S. Truman is a prime instance. His extemporaneous utterances often had the kind of vigor, strength, and cogency that many of his more formal speeches, prepared with a good deal of care (with the assistance of executive aides, no doubt) and carefully read from manuscript, seemed to lack.

This difference between two types of oral presentation brings us to one of the public address critic's omnipresent problems, the authenticity of materials. Literary critics are not confronted with this difficulty or, at least, seem not to be worried about it. It is assumed that the novel or poem, or even the essay is truly the work of the author. This is accepted even though editors and assistants may have had a hand in the completed work. With contemporary speechmaking, almost everyone is aware of the significant role that ghost writers and speech writers play in making the busy public servant more loquacious, if not more articulate. It is up to the critic to ascertain the extent of the speech writer's role in the speaker's development. Much has been written on the authenticity and even the reporting of contemporary speeches. Congressional speeches, in particular, whose complete texts supposedly appear in the *Congressional Record*, are not always the speeches given on the floor of Congress. Additions are often made to them; deletions and modifications take place before they appear in print. One need only study the same speech as reported in *Vital Speeches, The New York Times*, and the *Congressional Record* to see some of the differences. The student of public address, as well as the embryonic critic, should be aware of this pitfall and take it into serious consideration in his own description and analysis of a particular speech.

The critic of public address is confronted with other difficulties. He must decide whether or not to use other than classical standards in the analysis of formal elements of oratory. It is easy to trod well-worn paths in analyzing a particular speech. It is much more difficult, but perhaps more rewarding, to utilize more contemporary or even completely new measuring devices. Often if new visions of truth are to be given by the critic, it must be accomplished uniquely and creatively. Creativity may be stifled, rather than enhanced, by using the same well-worn, tired tools.

Irving J. Lee, in an interesting and provocative article called "Four Ways of Looking at a Speech"[1] in the *Quarterly Journal of Speech*, provides some fresher views and standards. Lee indicates that the formulations of the rhetoricians—especially the classical ones—while useful for analysis, have been stressed to an inordinate degree. His own suggestions are divided into three major categories (in addition to those coming from the rhetoricians). They are those emanating from such diverse disciplines as semantics, which is related to signification or meaning; logic, the probing of evidence and reasoning; and general semantics, an attempt at scientific analysis of blocks to communication and understanding. Professor Lee is a prime and articulate exponent of the last. His explication of the method of general semantics is cogent as well as utilitarian. The concepts have since been found useful by some analysts and critics.

Lee's methods can be jumping off points for the creative critic, who can devise standards to adjust or even cater to the modern temper. Occasionally a journal or periodical article does contain some innovations in method and process of descriptive analysis in speechmaking. This is far too infrequent, however, for the growth and vitality of public address criticism. Martin Maloney, however, does propose such an innovation in "Some New Directions in Rhetorical Criticism," which appeared in the *Central States Speech Journal*.[2] Maloney's emphasis is upon the descriptive and inductive in speech criticism as against the present method, which he believes to be evaluative and deductive. His proposals might prove helpful to the nascent critic. They are quantitative analysis, of a content nature; qualitative content analysis; figurative analysis; and intonational analysis. By using this approach, Maloney believes speech criticism could become research into certain kinds of human behavior.

Another theorist who suggests more emphasis upon content analysis is W. Charles Redding. His piece entitled "Extrinsic and Intrinsic Criticism" appeared in *Western Speech*.[3] Redding explains that content analysis is simply a close examination, sentence by sentence, of any oral or written discourse. Its purpose is to determine what kinds of "meanings" are represented by the words. Essentially, it is an elaborate semantic analysis of symbols. Redding proposes that content analysis be used by the public address critic because it is a powerful instrument in the comprehension of what the speaker has to say.

The nascent critic, looking for new methodologies, needs to be wary. Occasionally, new measuring devices for analysis are proposed for the sake of innovation alone. The theorist may do so, not so much because he believes the new approach is the best one or that it has unique uses, but that it will give him a hearing more rapidly. Such ventures into critical theory are inexcusable. Fortunately, in rhetoric there are very few.

But the critic, looking for new approaches, should also be wary for another reason. It is usually not advisable to commit oneself to a theory and then apply it, "come hell or high water." This can be disastrous. The tools will not necessarily be useful for working the material.

Instead, the critic should be certain that the criteria

used are appropriate to the speech. In analysis some general discernments can be made by utilizing the well-advised tools. But perhaps more specific ones, for describing and analyzing both content and form, can be devised for a particular genre, if not for a particular speech.

Poems, plays, essays, and novels are all written communication and expression. The literary critic would be naive indeed if he were to scrutinize and analyze these different forms by using the same literary canons. So, too, with the informative speech, the learned lecture, the sermon, the eulogy, or the political address. While these are all oral communication and expression, would it not be wise for the rhetorical critic to differentiate among them by devising standards uniquely fitted to the particular form? Undoubtedly the resulting description and analysis would prove more fruitful.

Should Jonathan Edwards' great sermon, "God Glorified in Man's Dependence," be explicated and analyzed or even generally discussed by the same hallmarks as Abraham Lincoln's "Gettysburg Address?" Should the same standards be used in examining a press conference by President Lyndon B. Johnson as in scrutinizing an after-dinner speech by that debunker, C. Northcote Parkinson? Certainly not. Yet much analytical description of oral utterances is accomplished in the same monotonous old-fashioned way. Is it any wonder, then, that our studies rarely reach beyond the confines of our own little academic rhetorical community? Is it any wonder that they often are not given much credence by scholars in other disciplines? Is it any wonder, in fact, that much of what passes for criticism of public address reaches the layman through literary figures or journalists? Not that they do not have something to offer. As a matter of fact, we can learn from "Lessons from the Literary Critics," as Robert D. Clark points out in a recent essay in *Western Speech*.[4] Clark explains that a number of literary formulations can be used by the rhetorical critic. Among these, the New Criticism, the close scrutiny of a literary text, stands high. But perhaps most important in the piece is the idea that public address critics use the following important analogue from literature: that criticism, in the general sense, is any intelligent discussion of literature.

What the public address critic must eventually do then, is study the individual speech itself: its genre, its particular aim, its ramifications, its unique qualities. Then he should decide on the particular tools he will use for description and analysis. Through this inductive method he will best accomplish his aim. He will not accomplish it in an exemplary fashion by applying to a speech the same outward criteria, whether fitting or not. Only in this manner can the critic make an effective contribution to knowledge, and add to the vivacity and vitality of speech criticism.

The more traditional methods of speech description and analysis can still bear fruit. There are a number of these valuable tools, as A. Craig Baird indicates in his introduction to the volume of *American Public Addresses, 1740–1952*. In it he subdivides the study of speeches into a number of useful categories, all relevant for analysis.[5]

Some of these have been used with lucidity and eclat by the critics of public address. One is the fine study of Jeremiah S. Black by William Norwood Brigance, appearing in Volume I of the *History and Criticism of American Public Address* series. Here is how Brigance dealt with the problems of writing, speaking, and invective. The last, of course, is an important ingredient in the use of extra-logical appeal by Black:

> Throughout life he was a prolific controversial writer, engaging at times Stephen A. Douglas, James A. Garfield, Charles Francis Adams, Henry Wilson, and Robert G. Ingersoll; and in these writings he gained fame as a dangerous adversary. Yet his speeches, as they come unrevised from his lips, are superior in style to his controversial articles that were carefully written and revised. Like the poet and the prophet, he thought more profoundly and phrased more eloquently when impassioned. But with him passion came not in the sequestered calm of the study but in the heat of forensic combat.
>
> His invective was at times compared with that of Swift and repeatedly with that of Junius. It is true he used invective with terrible power, but he used it cautiously in the courtroom. In controversial writing it was his commonplace weapon, for here he delighted to "have at" his victim,

and that seemed to be his only goal. Not so when he spoke. Before him was the court, which he, as a former judge, held always in deep respect. He had in view a decision to be won, and he allowed no uncontrolled language to injure his efforts. True, he used invective before courts; but his sarcasm was syllogistic and was seasoned with anecdote until even the victim seldom bore malice.

Toward the court there was a fearlessness in his manner that gained him the reputation of being allowed greater freedom of utterance than any other living man at the bar. Yet, basically, his attitude toward the court was one of deep respect. He himself was an ex-judge. He revered the judiciary; . . .[6]

Robert G. Gunderson, too, gives us some useful and penetrating visions into the speaking of Daniel Webster at a specific time, the 1840 presidential campaign, when the "Godlike Daniel" supported William Henry Harrison. In his piece, "Webster in Linsey-Woolsey," Gunderson describes and analyzes the adaptations which Webster made during the so-called "Log Cabin Campaign." The few excerpts following should give us an inkling of the many facets involved in the analysis. First, Gunderson writes, Webster divested himself of his usual elegant clothing; then:

... the Godlike Daniel donned a linsey-woolsey coat, a wide-brimmed hat, knee-high boots, and a flowing necktie, and set out on a stumping expedition which took him from the crest of Mount Stratton in Vermont to the steps of the State Capitol in Richmond, Virginia. To identify himself with the new coonskin Whiggery, Webster camped with Green Mountain boys in a pine wood before an open fire, ate meals from shingles, paid tribute to log cabins, and challenged at fisticuffs anyone who dared call him an aristocrat.[7]

On entering the uproarious log cabin and hard cider campaign for "Tippecanoe and Tyler Too," Webster was forced to make changes in his classical delivery. In his extemporaneous speaking, he adopted a manner which some have described as "conversational". . . . His extemporaneous speeches varied from one to three and one-half hours and caused him much physical discomfort. . . . Late in October, after he had talked for three hours in a cold rain at Francestown, New Hampshire, severe influenza silenced his voice for the remainder of the canvass.

Though contemporary newspapers made frequent references to Webster's voice and his illnesses, there were few specific comments about his gestures. Yet enemies as well as friends paid tribute to his oratorical ability.[8]

Webster adapted his style as well as his delivery to that which pleased convention-goers of 1840. As one sympathetic contemporary put it, "Some men of the highest culture did not disdain to go down to the people. . . ." With something of this spirit of condescension, Webster used language which was often "crisp and colloquial, rich in homely idioms and humorous turns of phrase." Some of his epigrams became campaign rallying cries. "We have fallen, gentlemen," he proclaimed at Baltimore, "upon *hard times*, and the remedy seems to be HARD CIDER."

When on the stump Webster often used classical allusions which, no doubt, were more impressive than meaningful to noisy, cider-soaked audiences. . . . But no matter how unfamiliar his allusions, flattered audiences responded with applause.

Webster knew the devices as well as the language which influenced the voter. He made frequent and effective use of rhetorical questions; and, at times, he invited overt audience response. . . .

During the canvass, Senator Webster, the great exponent of federalism, tailored his subject matter to his specific audience. Campaigning for the first time south of the Potomac, he developed a new respect for States' Rights. In appearances at Alexandria and Richmond, the Massachusetts Senator responded to Southern hospitality by avoiding subjects such as the tariff and the bank. At Alexandria, amid aquatic displays and "the roar of cannon and musketry," he declared: "We of New England are bound to you by our sacred compact the Constitution of the United States." Minor differences between Northern and Southern Whigs, he thought, could be settled without the help of Loco-Foco Democrats. . . . By implication, therefore, Northern and Southern Whigs were doing battle against an enemy scarcely less odious than George III.[9]

In order to illustrate the various aspects of Webster's speechmaking, I have used only Gunderson's analytical conclusions. He supports these statements, to be sure, with a multitudinous flow of specific quotations from Webster's speeches and contemporary newspapers. As a matter of fact, Gunderson's article of less than eight pages cites seventy-two footnotes coming from original, as well as secondary sources. Such is the price of scholarly rhetorical description and analysis.

To illustrate the relationship between preparation and presentation, we can study William A. Behl's scholarly monograph, "Theodore Roosevelt's Principles of Speech Preparation and Delivery."[10] Written about twenty years ago, it is a fine example of describing and analyzing these salient factors in the orator's art. And Carroll C. Arnold's "Invention in the Parliamentary Speaking of Benjamin Disraeli, 1842–1852"[11] is an effective exposition of this first canon in the speaking of one of Britain's greatest 19th century orators.

There are many other useful studies on the descriptive and analytical level, either of particular ingredients in speechmaking or of a particular speech. Rhetorical scholars do fine work in these realms, and the journals are full of such studies. Wayne C. Eubank's effective essay entitled "Benjamin Morgan Palmer's Lottery Speech, New Orleans, 1891"[12] might be looked at. Here, as in some genuinely creative and critical works, there is a fine blending of description and analysis, and interpretation and evaluation. This the student can study for his own erudition and enjoyment.

The student and practitioner of public address criticism can find a great deal of material to study and use as exemplars of the accepted classical methods of descriptive analysis. The three volumes of the *History and Criticism of American Public Address* is one source. The speech journals—national and regional—are another. But for other newer, and perhaps more useful approaches to contemporary speaking, the critic can only depend on himself.

QUESTIONS AND PROJECTS

1. Write an analysis of the ideas and proofs in Kennedy's Inaugural Address.

2. Describe and analyze the use of style in Eugene McCarthy's address nominating Adlai Stevenson for the Presidency at the 1960 Democratic convention.
3. Write an essay analyzing a speech given by a character in a fictional literary work (novel, play, etc.). Political novels especially provide fruitful sources.
4. Describe the organizational format of a recent speech published in *Vital Speeches*.
5. Write a paper assessing the relative importance of the classical canons of oratory for modern criticism.
6. Outline the criteria you would use for the analysis of a sermon. How would these differ from those for a political address? How would they differ from a formal expository lecture?
7. Hubert H. Humphrey is considered a prolific and effective orator. Write a descriptive analysis of one of his speeches with the emphasis on his invention.

NOTES

1. Irving J. Lee, "Four Ways of Looking at a Speech," *Quarterly Journal of Speech*, XXVI, 2 (April, 1942), 148–155.
2. Martin Maloney, "Some New Directions in Rhetorical Criticism," *Central States Speech Journal*, IV, 3 (March, 1953), 1–5.
3. W. Charles Redding, "Extrinsic and Intrinsic Criticism," *Western Speech*, XXI, 2 (Spring, 1957), 96–103.
4. Robert D. Clark, "Lessons from the Literary Critics," *Western Speech*, XXI, 2 (Spring, 1957), 83–89.
5. A. Craig Baird, *American Public Addresses, 1740–1952* (New York: McGraw-Hill, 1956), pp. 1–14.
6. William Norwood Brigance, "Jeremiah S. Black," in *History and Criticism of American Public Address*, William N. Brigance, ed. (New York: McGraw-Hill, 1943), Vol. I, pp. 474–475.
7. Robert G. Gunderson, "Webster in Linsey-Woolsey," *Quarterly Journal of Speech*, XXXVII, 1 (February, 1951), 23.
8. *Ibid.*, p. 24.
9. *Ibid.*, pp. 25–26.
10. William A. Behl, "Theodore Roosevelt's Principles of

Speech Preparation and Delivery," *Speech Monographs,* Vol. XII (1945), 112–122.

11. Carroll C. Arnold, "Invention in the Parliamentary Speaking of Benjamin Disraeli, 1842–1852," *Speech Monographs,* Vol. XIV (1947), 66–80.

12. Wayne C. Eubank, "Benjamin Morgan Palmer's Lottery Speech, New Orleans, 1891," *Southern Speech Journal,* XXIV, 1 (Fall, 1958), 2–15.

SELECTED BIBLIOGRAPHY

Baird, A. Craig, "The Study of Speeches," *American Public Addresses, 1740–1952,* New York: McGraw-Hill, 1956.

Cain, Earl R., "A Method for Rhetorical Analysis of Congressional Debate," *Western Speech,* XVIII, 2 (March, 1954), 91–95.

Clark, Robert D., "Lessons from the Literary Critics," *Western Speech,* XXI, 2 (Spring, 1957), 83–89.

Lee, Irving J., "Four Ways of Looking at a Speech," *Quarterly Journal of Speech,* XXVI, 2 (April, 1942), 148–155.

Maloney, Martin, "Some New Directions in Rhetorical Criticism," *Central States Speech Journal,* IV, 3 (March, 1953), 1–5.

Richardson, Ralph, "A Suggestion for a Project in Contemporary Criticism," *Western Speech,* XIX, 1 (January, 1955), 5–8.

Thompson, Wayne, "Contemporary Public Address: A Problem in Criticism," *Quarterly Journal of Speech,* XL, 1 (February, 1954), 24–30.

Thonssen, Lester and A. Craig Baird, *Speech Criticism,* New York: Ronald Press, 1948.

Western Speech, XXI, 2 (Spring, 1957). This whole issue is a symposium on criticism and public address. The guest editor is Ernest J. Wrage.

8 *Interpretation and Evaluation of Speechmaking*

Logically, interpretation and evaluation should follow the description and analysis of a speech or address. Often the critique itself is an amalgam of all these components. It is not subdivided neatly into the two former objective elements and the two latter more subjective ones. Critical writing is of a piece. Rather artificial demarcations provide an aid in seeing the discrete elements. They are not suggested as a method for writing. In learning his art, the critic should be able to discern and differentiate these elements, but he should not be tied to them in a finished critique. Fact and interpretation, while theoretically different in scope and method, are inextricably interwoven in the actual critical assessment. This blending adds the individual creative touch which, if lacking, makes the piece not a work of art but a mediocre written exercise. This exercise may be useful as a preliminary study, but it hardly has value as finished criticism.

For criticism of public address must be considered an art form. As such, one cannot press a button in a scientific manner and expect useful and effective critical results. It may be that too much of our criticism attempts to follow this pseudo-scientific procedure. It may be, too, that this is the reason it lacks vivacity, vitality, and merit. For while description and analysis, as the more objective methods, utilize a somewhat scientific method, interpretation and evaluation seldom do. As the more subjective and perhaps creative components, they tend to follow artistic rather than scientific canons.

We are now concerned with a difficult aspect of public

address criticism. This is the complex problem of individual interpretation and assessment of all the particulars of the speech itself. While it is related generally to the interpretation and evaluation of the ideas, views, and philosophy of the particular speaker, as discussed in Chapter Six, it should be differentiated in the realm of content and form.

In a previous chapter, suggestions were made for explicating, analyzing, interpreting, and criticizing the general ideas of a speaker. In this chapter, the suggestions concern the specific ideas of a particular speech, and then are related to the speaker's general views when this relationship is appropriate.

Perhaps even more significant than the critical consideration of content or invention is the interpretation and assessment of salient elements of form. And most important is the relation and integration of form and content for the purpose of discovering how the facets of form and the artistic elements of structure and style affected the content of a particular speech.

Because interpretation is an artistic endeavor, no two persons would interpret an oratorical work in exactly the same way. The literature of public address is replete with examples. A comparatively recent one makes the point.

A great furor was raised at the end of the 1964 Republican Convention in San Francisco with Senator Barry Goldwater's speech accepting the Republican Presidential nomination. This furor was created when Goldwater said: "I would remind you that extremism in the defense of liberty is no vice . . . also . . . moderation in the pursuit of justice is no virtue!"[1] There immediately began attacks, explanations, questions, and justifications.

The attacks, which came from two sources, were mostly on the term "extremism," its interpretation and ramifications. The first attacks came from the so-called Republican moderates, Governor Nelson Rockefeller of New York, Governor George Romney of Michigan, and others. Later they came from the Democratic opposition. This, to be sure, came during the actual campaign rather than during the convention.

The explanations came from members of Senator Goldwater's staff, who attempted to give a general definition of "extremism" and its implications. The definition implied favorable connotations.

The questions came from such notable figures in the Republican party as Richard M. Nixon. In a letter to Goldwater, which was made public, Nixon asked some questions about the same provocative term, "extremism." General Dwight D. Eisenhower, too, was confused and asked for a clarification of the controversial term.

The justification came from Goldwater himself. He requested an audience with Eisenhower to justify the use of the term, its interpretation, and its possible ramifications. The Senator explained to the General that extreme action, in the Senator's view, would be quite similar to the kind of extreme action that Eisenhower took on the beaches at Normandy. General Eisenhower accepted the explanatory justification. He stated that he had not originally seen it that way, but now he was satisfied. In this manner Barry Goldwater justified the use of the term to Eisenhower, and probably to many others, since the exchange between the two Republican leaders was well publicized.

This short example only illustrates the magnitude of the task of interpretation. It is exceptionally difficult when unusual or extraordinary terms are used. How would a public address critic interpret the controversial phrases? Should his interpretation be dependent on the justifications and explanations of Goldwater and his staff? Should it depend on the interpretations—quite hostile, to be sure —of the opposition, the Democrats? Or should it depend on the critic's interpretation alone? Would the critic's interpretation make any difference in the eventual assessment and criticism of the address? Obviously, it would. For while Goldwater's speech and statements may be an extreme example of "extremism" needing interpretation, it is far from an isolated case.

Most critics who have spent any time at all in following political speechmaking know that the language and style follow certain general patterns. Political theorists, too, are aware of these factors. Jeremy Bentham, the founder of the English Utilitarian school of philosophy, wrote the *Handbook of Political Fallacies*,[2] which is one of the early exposés of the political and rhetorical tactics used by politicians. He focuses upon and explains such fallacies as authority, danger, delay, and confusion.

While generalizations are omnipresent in political speeches, specifics are often missing. There are various reasons for this absence. Perhaps the paramount one is that the appeal of specifics is often too small, individual, and, hence, hardly universal. When the political orator makes saintly references to God, country, or Constitution, or utilizes some of the above-mentioned fallacies, he is using broad, general, abstract terms often more for their emotional tone and impact than for intellectual erudition.

Another reason for the paucity of specifics is that speeches filled with generalities are easier to prepare and to present. Little time is needed for the speaker or his staff to do research. All that is needed are a few generalizations supported by other generalizations, and a speech is composed.

Strangely enough, the general address often has more appeal for an audience than an explicit one. Audiences do not like to follow the intricacies of a closely reasoned argument filled with explicit details, whose ramifications they cannot easily grasp. Much better are the simple exhortations, the time proven crowd pleasers, and the political clichés. Almost every politician knows these by heart, and uses them whenever the occasion appears. Rhetorically, there is more than a modicum of merit in this procedure. This is particularly true if results are the measure of effectiveness of the talk.

There is another significant reason for the use of general appeals. Since the interpretation of a speech is largely an individual affair, the more general the utterance, the wider the potential appeal may be. Each member of the audience can fit the generalization to his own ideas and experiences. And if the speaker realizes intuitively that the audience supplies their own explicit details for the speaker's general suggestions, he will rely more on generalizations than on specifics. Moreover, often these generalities are purposely unsupported so that the specifics can be filled in by the auditors. And, as every rhetorician knows, this is the best way for an auditor to persuade himself.

The audience in the San Francisco Cow Palace who heard the Goldwater phrases on extremism made of them what they would. Since most of them were somewhat conversant with the ultra-conservative views of the Senator from Arizona, they probably took the phrase to mean that extreme conservative measures (which many liked) would be used to run the country if Goldwater were to be elected. They thus persuaded themselves. But this persuasion was accomplished within the framework of the Senator's suggestions, and they, therefore, heartily applauded the candidate.

The audiences listening via radio and television were certainly not as homogeneous politically or socially as the audience in San Francisco. They probably did not interpret the "extremism" phrases in quite the same way. Some may have been frightened by the implications. Some may have been gratified. Others may have been elated. Still others probably considered it campaign oratory; remained cynical, phlegmatic, and unmoved. It may be that even Goldwater, the articulator and circulator of those words, was not fully cognizant of the potential furor and ramifications of the phrases. Or he may have been completely aware of their powerful impact and used them for the effect they would make. Moreover, unless there is evidence to the contrary, this latter view must be accepted as the position of the speaker. Orators speak to persuade.

What of the critic in this situation? What will his reaction be? How will he get to the real essence of such terms? How will he know the "truth"? To assume that there is one absolute, universal interpretation would be naive, if not false. Nevertheless, if the critic is worth his salt, he must try to unearth the essential truth of the terms. He will do this by going to the speech itself, describing and analyzing not only these terms, but all of the others. Then he will examine all of its components from the standpoint of content and form. Only then will he be in a position to interpret the meaning of abstract and nebulous words. If this kind of probing still does not satisfy him, the critic will also go to the man himself. He will study his ideas and philosophy. He will look at his views as articulated in other speeches and writings. He will compare, contrast, weigh, and analyze. Only then will he come to some conclusions.

While the focus thus far has been on political persuasive speaking and its interpretation, much the same difficulty exists in other kinds of speechmaking. Take religious speaking as an example. The relative difficulty of interpretation here quite obviously depends on the speaker, his subject, and his audience. Not all religious speaking is highly esoteric for the layman. If it were, the churches would not house many listeners and participants during their services. Nevertheless, some of it is. For the sake of an elementary explanation, religious speaking can be divided into a simple-complex dichotomy. Probably, much of such speaking is on some line between these two extremes.

Norman Vincent Peale, the celebrated minister and exponent of positive thinking, occupies one end of this simple-complex spectrum. His method is to use numerous examples and illustrations to explicate a text, or to lend force to his views. This makes the problem of interpretation both for the audience and the critic less difficult. His lectures, sermons, and writings are, therefore, instantly intelligible to listeners and readers. In one respect, this makes Peale a very popular lecturer and writer for lay audiences. His simplifications, over-simplifications according to some critics, make the listening and reading audience believe that almost anything is possible. Moreover, the critic, examining and interpreting his speeches, preparatory to criticizing them, experiences little difficulty in the process.

This is not the case with the late Paul Tillich, minister, noted theologian, professor, and proponent of existentialism. He would probably be placed on the other end of the simple-complex spectrum of difficulty of understanding and interpretation. Tillich's lectures and sermons were concerned with such abstractions as love, power, and justice, and their relevancy for today's world. Several factors militate against easy comprehension and artistic elucidation of Tillich's utterances. First, he did not offer simple solutions to complex problems. His erudition and the depth of his thought in theological concepts is a second factor. Third, and related to the first and second, difficult theological formulations cannot be explained in simple language and style. These are but a few of the reasons for the complexity of Tillich. It is true that Tillich, like Norman Vincent Peale, also attempted to facilitate comprehension of his ideas by the utilization of specific illustrations. But these are neither so numerous nor as simple as those of Peale. The problem is compounded in the case of Tillich because he was not a native born American, and his idiom was more that of his German forebears than of his adopted country. His language and style are unusual and generally difficult. This formal problem, added to Tillich's esoteric concepts, presents some difficulties of more than average magnitude for the critic.

All that has been discussed so far about the interpretation of speechmaking has concerned the rhetorical elements. The social problems of interpretation add further difficulty. The critic may well ask himself what meaning his interpretation of the speech or lecture has for society. His answer to that question makes him not only a rhetorical critic, but a social one as well. In other words, he becomes a critic of public address with all its multitudinous ramifications. The critic should be constantly aware of this serious responsibility. No speaker speaks in a vacuum; he speaks within a climate of opinion. The easy generalizations of Norman Vincent Peale are accepted much more widely and readily today than the more difficult formulations of Paul Tillich, although the climate may be changing. The public address critic is part of a social construct and operates within the times and circumstances of that construct. He has social as well as rhetorical duties. His role as a critic can enlarge and enhance this dual function, provided he accepts the responsibility. There are, then, possible social as well as rhetorical implications to be considered in the critic's interpretation.

If the process of artistic and social elucidation—whether

of a Goldwater or a Tillich—sometimes presents infinite problems because of elements in both content and form, think how much more difficult is the last step taken by the critic. Evaluation, assessment, and criticism involve judgment that is complex and hard to apply. This should make the critic more aware of that judgment and more eager to accept all the ramifications of his judgment. Critical scholarship can unearth facts about a speaker; describe the salient facets of speech, setting, and audience; and explicate, analyze, and interpret the speech. The highest role to which the critic can aspire is the passing of judgment. This is what he has been preparing for throughout much of his rhetorical and social training. To judge the facts of a speech or a speaker is useful but not enough. Not to use this preparation for analysis and interpretation is a fault indeed; not to use it for criticism is almost an artistic heresy.

When the formal and content aspects of a speech are being evaluated, the speech must be carefully scrutinized. Every significant word must be examined for its possible implications and relationships to other words. Every meaningful phrase must be probed for ramifications and relations to other phrases. Every sentence, every paragraph, every page must be dealt with in a similar manner. At this stage of evaluation, the scrutiny is not only for the purpose of interpretation. This has already been accomplished. Now the public address critic begins to judge. Here, he says, the speaker's content was insignificant or significant, mediocre, good, excellent, superb. Here the speaker fell short of his objective. Here his ideas are general, or fallacious, or magnificent. Here his style impedes content; here it implements it. Here his reasoning is weak, or outstanding, or merely run of the mill. Here organization and arrangement follow a certain pattern especially fitted for the speaker's particular task; or it seems to be particularly incongruous if audience and occasion are considered. Here his preparation seems niggardly; his presentation prosaic or laconic, demonstrative or dramatic; fulsome or sparse, passionate or sober, humorous or mock serious. And what of all this? Is this good, bad, mediocre, average, excellent, superb? Is the speaker a fool, a clown, a leader, a statesman, a contributor to society? Why? What of comparisons and contrasts with other speakers in like situations? Does the present speaker measure up to them or fall by the wayside?

It is not enough to say, for instance, that the speaker under consideration was the best orator of his generation. Many orators have been given such an accolade. But what of the reasons for it? Is he a good enough speaker so that future generations can read his utterances with profit? Should they? Why? Should they read it because of his ideas; because of style; because of argument; because of passion?

By now the student of public address criticism is aware that there is very little of this kind of judgment to be found in the assessment of American public address. It is not easy to do, and the critic is hesitant to have to justify himself to the critical community and the world. Very few individuals take on this task, whether in the rhetorical or the literary worlds.

Yvor Winters, Stanford professor and literary critic, is one of the few who manage to deal with this responsibility. His creative judgments have appeared in scholarly publications for many years. Not an *enfant terrible* like Leslie Fiedler, Winters is an accomplished literary scholar and critic who is not averse to exercising moral judgments upon writers and especially poets. Stanley Edgar Hyman has called him our foremost representative of Johnsonian criticism, in which evaluation is the crowning glory of critical analysis. Yvor Winters fulfills that appellation by his critiques of Hart Crane, T. S. Eliot, John Crowe Ransom, Edward Arlington Robinson, and Robert Frost.[3] The critic of public address would do well to read some of Winters' works to see how he accomplishes the evaluative role.

Another evaluative critic, unafraid of commitment to judgment, is the previously mentioned Leslie Fiedler. Mr. Fiedler rambles all over the literary and social landscape, almost like a bull in a china shop according to some, but a highly moral and ethical critic according to others. He has published extensively. *No! in Thunder*[4] and *Love and*

Death in the American Novel[5] are particularly useful. His works have a verve and flavor that make them a delight to read, whether one agrees with his assessments or not. But they also show Fiedler engaged with judgment and criticism in the fullest sense.

Only recently Edward Dahlberg, considered by some to be one of the most neglected writers of American literature, has taken on the task of criticism. In *Alms for Oblivion*,[6] Dahlberg illustrates that he is the sharpest serious critic today, and probably the most necessary. In this study he dissects such reverential works as *Moby Dick* and *The Great Gatsby* so as to shake the reader loose from his accustomed habit and indolence.

While some literary critics are not afraid of dissecting the literary works and their writers in this fashion, fewer public address critics are willing to do the same. Barnet Baskerville has given us an example in his study of Joseph McCarthy,[7] originally read at a Speech Association of America convention, and later published. Baskerville, writing at a time when McCarthyism literally threatened America, analyzed and evaluated the specious and sophistic utterances of the then Senator from Wisconsin. Baskerville's summary overview of some contemporary evangelists of the far right—Dr. Frederick Schwarz, Dr. Billy James Hargis, and Dr. Carl McIntire—also provide penetrating discernments into the rhetoric of these staunch upholders of the everlasting fight of Christianity against Communism. The essay, noted for its bold and forthright tone, appeared in *Western Speech*.[8]

Bower Aly also illustrates the faculty of seeing into the inner character and underlying truth in the speaking of certain orators. Professor Aly, who has become nationally known as a Hamiltonian scholar, takes up arms in defense of Alexander Hamilton. Aly felt that unjustified strictures have too often been made about Hamilton. Aly's assessment puts Hamilton, as man and speaker, in a more favorable light than he has often been seen before by foe and friend alike.[9] The rhetorical-social method of Aly's evaluation is a useful model for those who are convinced that public address serves society in a constantly evolving cultural framework. He suggests by his criticism his concern with our cultural and social history as conditioning and conditioned by American speakers.

Some critics have not agreed with Aly's assessment, and have suggested other, perhaps more condemnatory, views. It seems to me, for example, that:

> . . . Alexander Hamilton was an orator, statesman and politician whose ideas on democracy and the people were formed by looking over past history, there to discover that man was essentially incapable of self-government; and this was largely due to ignorance, selfishness and lack of self-control. This idea of the incompetence of man manifested itself in both his philosophic cogitations and articulations, and in his attempts to put theory into practice.
>
> From this philosophic viewpoint, since he did not believe that human nature, as he had observed it in the past, would change in the future, he could only conclude that the common man, to put it mildly, was untrustworthy. Hence, he felt an inherent dislike for democratic processes.
>
> Practically he tried to put this theory into the law of the land when he attempted to deny political equality to the people by removing them as far as possible from political power. This was to be accomplished by making the national government a stronger one through the utilization of the following: first, the executive was to hold office for life, or during good behavior; second, senators would also hold office in the same manner as the president; third, both the president and the senators would be chosen by electors, rather than by the people; and finally, the people themselves would choose the electors. These ideas, if they had been put into practice, would have insured a strong government, administered by a ruling hierarchy, thus leaving the people out of direct political participation. To this end, too, it has been seen during the election of 1800, that he was prepared to take measures which were much stronger than mere talk.
>
> Couple to all the above Hamilton's conceptions of the importance of property, and his work for the upholding of government by "the rich, the wise, and the well-born," and one can only conclude that he was against the idea of both the humanness and the humaneness of man. It thus is not difficult to assert that the prevailing attitude about the character and good will of Hamilton—about

his ethos in short—is the correct one. Is it any wonder then, that the job of cleansing him is more than difficult, and that "the liberals . . . have despised Hamilton and the conservatives have rejected him?"[10]

Evaluating Alexander Hamilton as man and speaker suggests the importance that political and social criteria might have had in setting up standards for analysis and assessment. This does not mean, however, that critics of public address should consider only their own political and social standards, or only partisan factors in their eventual assessment of a controversial figure such as Hamilton. What often happens is that different critics view the orator—and Hamilton is a prime example—not only from different political and social perspectives, but from different rhetorical perspectives as well. As a result, they come up with divergent evaluations from somewhat similar data and sometimes even from somewhat similar analyses of that data. This emphasizes the magnitude of the problem that evaluation poses for the critic of public address. In assessment, the critic attempts to utilize all of the evidence, the analysis, and the interpretation. Then by a leap of his mind, rationally and intuitively, he comes to some definitive judgment. It must be remembered that judgment of an orator is not made on ideological grounds alone, interesting and useful as these are. What compounds the difficulty of judgment is the necessity of using both formal and content elements in the eventual assessment. Moreover, as any public address critic worth his salt knows, these are not separated in the speech in quite the same way that rhetorical theory suggests. Form implements content; content formulates form.

Evaluations of this type, using both social and rhetorical criteria, are quite often made of less controversial as well as highly controversial figures of the American political scene. Take Thomas Jefferson as an example. Not viewed as a great orator and, hence, not deemed worthy of much rhetorical analysis, Jefferson has been found to be a highly competent speaker. To be sure, this depends on the measuring devices used in the criticism. If rhetorical standards are used exclusively, we get one kind of evaluation. "The usual view is that weakness in delivery and an inward turning scholarly nature, despite his excellences in invention and style caused him to shun the platform and to be ineffective on it."[11]

Jefferson was, however, in another view, an impressive speaker who could hold the attention of the audience.[12] "In his speechmaking, Jefferson used diverse styles which he suited to the audience and the occasion. The sonorous periods of his First Inaugural are quite different from the simple sentences of his addresses to the Indians. Such versatility, though no doubt arising primarily in the qualities of mind, was also a product of his combining a classical background with a long study of the Indians and their languages."[13]

If we use criteria of a moral and social as well as rhetorical nature, however, the assessment is of a different kind. To be sure, "Jefferson was more inclined to use the persuasive process and more skillful in its employment than has been believed in the past. In dealing with the Indians he adapted intelligently to the occasion and audience, employed his ethical advantages, skillfully showed good judgment in arrangement and in control over length, and combined logical and emotional appeals with a shrewd view to his true, long-range objectives. Finally, he played skillfully on the nuance value of words as his own policies and corresponding speech purposes were altered."[14]

But "Moral standards should be part of the critical apparatus; and if they are, Jefferson must be condemned for being less than consistent when his words to the red men are compared with his actions. . . . The shifting position of Jefferson here is not consistent with the stalwart democratic image which in his own time and in our present day adds so much to the impact of his pronouncements. . . . [Finally] what Jefferson loses in stature as an idealist, he possibly makes up as a practical orator using invention, style and presentation in the service of practical political ends."[15]

The student, then, can find examples of evaluative criticism among the critics of public address. It is not necessarily blatant, nor does it need to be. The rapier, when one must use it in criticism, can be more effective than the bludgeon. Nor should this suggest that all evaluative judgment need be critical in the derogatory sense. Fulsome praise, if deserved in the assessment of the critic, can be of as much value to those readers of criticism, seeking new and useful perceptions as is ironic derogation. Both can play significantly important roles in shaking up and awakening the readers from the throes of indolence and apathy. Evaluative criticism of this type is a necessity at all times.

If the critic of public address decides that evaluation is his forte, he must be prepared for castigation, if not ostracism. He must be willing to accept these strictures. He will be on sounder ground if he is aware that his judgments are not made lightly. He must be sure that ethical factors enter into his assessments. If he accepts the standard that the creative critical act is essentially a moral judgment and is aware of the possible implications and ramifications, his analyses and assessments will rest on a fairly solid foundation.

Nor should he feel remiss in reading and studying other than rhetorical critics to enhance his own understanding of how judgment and evaluation are used in criticism. This chapter has mentioned some literary critics whose evaluations are worthy of study. Other chapters have suggested that historians who take on the role of criticism can also be helpful. They can serve in one way as exemplars to the critic of public address. But social criticism, art criticism, dramatic criticism, perhaps even music criticism can be scrutinized to aid the rhetorical critic in discerning and evaluating the social, moral, and aesthetic factors in the criticism of public address. Not that the public address critic will use the same hallmarks for his own assessments; but he can see how they are used, and through relationships and analogy, his own judgments will be enhanced and made more meaningful.

QUESTIONS AND PROJECTS

1. Write a paper on William Lowndes Yancey's "For Southern Rights." Examine and evaluate carefully the rhetorical

and social implications of the speech, and how content and form are welded into one whole for maximum effect.

2. Do the same as above for Robert M. La Follette's "Free Speech in Wartime."

3. Evaluate the content and form of Emerson's "The American Scholar," and relate this assessment to his transcendental philosophy. Do you agree, that given his ideas, the approach he used is the only one he could make? Why? If you do not agree, give an alternate rhetorical approach that he might have utilized.

4. Read an essay by a literary critic in which evaluative criticism is used and compare and contrast it with an essay you have read by a rhetorical critic who also utilized evaluative judgment. Write a paper in which you attempt to discern the bases for the criteria used by the two different types of critics.

5. When, if ever, is the public address critic correct in letting subjectivity creep into his rhetorical judgment? Write a short essay dealing with the ethical factors which are present in such a situation and how the critic should deal with them.

6. Write a short essay indicating how rhetorical criticism can implement social criticism.

7. Write a short paper indicating how social criticism can be of aid to the criticism of public address.

NOTES

1. Barry Goldwater, "Acceptance Address, Republican National Convention," *Vital Speeches*, XXX, 21 (August 21, 1964), 644.

2. Jeremy Bentham, *Handbook of Political Fallacies*, Harold A. Larabee, ed. (Baltimore, Maryland: Johns Hopkins Press, 1952).

3. Yvor Winters, *On Moderate Poets* (New York: Meridian Books, 1959).

4. Leslie Fiedler, *No! in Thunder* (Boston: Beacon Press), 1960).

5. ———, *Love and Death in the American Novel* (New York: Criterion Books, 1960).

6. Edward Dahlberg, *Alms for Oblivion* (Minneapolis: University of Minnesota Press, 1964).

7. Barnet Baskerville, "Joe McCarthy, Brief-Case Demagogue," *Today's Speech*, II, 3 (September, 1954), 8–15.

8. ———, "The Cross and the Flag: Evangelists of the Far Right," *Western Speech*, XXVII, 4 (Fall, 1963), 197–206.

9. Bower Aly, "Alexander Hamilton's Year," *Quarterly Journal of Speech*, XLIII, 4 (December, 1957), 427–432.

10. Anthony Hillbruner, "Invention and Ethos: The Metamorphosis of Alexander Hamilton," *Central States Speech Journal*, XI, 1 (Autumn, 1959), 46.

11. ———, "Word and Deed: Jefferson's Addresses to the Indians," *Speech Monographs*, XXX, 4 (November 1963), 328.

12. See Edmund Randolph, "Essay on the Revolutionary History of Virginia," *Virginia Magazine*, XLIII, p. 123, quoted in Marie Kimball, *The Road to Glory* (New York: Coward-McCann, 1943), p. 84.

13. Hillbruner, "Word and Deed: Jefferson's Addresses to the Indians," *op. cit.*, p. 329.

14. *Ibid.*, p. 333.

15. *Ibid.*, pp. 333–334.

SELECTED BIBLIOGRAPHY

Baskerville, Barnet, "Joe McCarthy, Brief-Case Demagogue," *Today's Speech*, II, 3 (September, 1954), 8–15.

———, "The Cross and the Flag: Evangelists of the Far Right," *Western Speech*, XXVII, 4 (Fall, 1963), 197–206.

Blau, Joseph L., "Public Address as Intellectual Revelation," *Western Speech*, XXI, 2 (Spring, 1957), 77–83.

Dahlberg, Edward, *Alms for Oblivion*, Minneapolis: University of Minnesota Press, 1964.

Fiedler, Leslie, *Love and Death in the American Novel*, New York: Criterion Books, 1960.

———, *No! In Thunder*, Boston: Beacon Press, 1960.

Hillbruner, Anthony, "Creativity in Contemporary Criticism," *Western Speech*, XXIV, 1 (Winter, 1960), 5–11.

———, "Criticism as Persuasion," *Southern Speech Journal*, XXVIII, 4 (Summer, 1963), 260–267.

———, "Invention and Ethos: The Metamorphosis of Alexander Hamilton," *Central States Speech Journal*, XI, 1 (Autumn, 1959), 41–48.

———, "The Rhetorical Critic's Role in Society," "Shop Talk," *Quarterly Journal of Speech*, XLIV, 1 (February, 1958), 100–102.

———, "Word and Deed: Jefferson's Addresses to the Indians," *Speech Monographs*, XXX, 4 (November, 1963), 328–334.

Hyman, Stanley Edgar, *The Armed Vision*, New York: Vintage Books, 1955.

Lomas, Charles W. "Agitator in a Cossack," *Western Speech*, XXVII, 1 (Winter, 1963), 16–24.

Nilson, Thomas, "Criticism and Social Consequences," *Quarterly Journal of Speech*, XLII, 2 (April, 1956), 173–178.

———, "Interpretative Function of the Critic," *Western Speech*, XXI, 2 (Spring, 1957), 70–76.

Redding, W. Charles, "Extrinsic and Intrinsic Criticism," *Western Speech*, XXI, 2 (Spring, 1957), 96–103.

Winters, Yvor, *On Modern Poets*, New York: Meridian Books, 1959.

9 The Functioning Critic

At this juncture, the student of public address criticism has seen that his art is not simple or negligible. In truth, it is complex as well as creative, objective as well as subjective, social as well as rhetorical, aesthetic as well as practical, and moral and ethical as well as relative and pragmatic. How can one art encompass all these factors and perhaps others which the critic will discover for himself? How can the critic, discovering the facts about a speech situation, analyzing and interpreting them, and passing judgment upon them, be relatively sure that he is correct in his assessments?

The art of public address, encompassing both social and rhetorical factors, is as complicated as life itself because it studies a medium of communication which concerns itself with every meaningful facet of life. And if public address is complex, it follows that its criticism will also be. Therefore, the student of public address and its criticism must be aware that he is a student of life in all its meaningful and sometimes unmeaningful ramifications and implications. The art of public address criticism attempts to deal with and judge the relationship of the art of oratory to life and man. Speech critics often feel this implicitly, and this awareness can add another dimension, another insight, another perspective to the concern that the critic has for man and society.

To the question of the critic's assurance that he is correct in his judgments, the answer is more complicated. Probably the first and most correct answer is that he is never sure. His judgments, so sure at one time, might be modified, altered, or changed by growth and development in his own discipline. Like the pursuit of life, the pursuit of criticism is an ever unfolding one. And like life itself, the critical perspectives gained at one stage may be completely different from those gained at another and more advanced stage. Commitment to one set of theories or standards may be effective for a certain time and place but not for another. In short, the critic can only be relatively sure—at any one moment of time—that the discernments he has gained and conveyed about a particular speech, speaker, or era in speaking are correct and have value. He can never have an absolute certainty about his assessments, any more than he can have an absolute surety that the life he leads is the correct one and, therefore, has value. In both cases, he has only a relative certainty; although, perhaps, there is more surety in the latter than in the former.

Does this mean that the critic must go through his career plagued by the question of whether he was right? Of course not. It is true that in criticism, as in life, there is indeed soul searching. But if either in criticism or in life there is so much constant questioning that the prime aim is lost sight of, then, indeed, the person has stopped functioning.

What the critic needs to do when confronted with such questioning is to be aware of the relativity of his judgments. He must also be aware of and focus on the synthetic factors of the functional criticism of public address.

The relativity of judgments does not mean that the critic is not engaged with his critical methods and analyses and committed to them. It means rather that given all the relevant material, and his own intellectual and critical acumen at the time, this is the best job of critical work that he can then accomplish. Given more data, more effective analysis, more experience, deeper discernment, and perhaps even a different or newer theoretical method, he should be aware that his judgments may be changed. Revision is always possible, often probable, and indeed necessary.

There should not be so little confidence in one's own judgments that there is constant and incessant revision going on during the critical process. Some of this is useful. However, there should not be so much as to prevent the communication of the results of the critical analysis. A critic must be a realist, not in the pejorative or opportunistic sense, but as one who realizes the constant flux of man and society. Then the critic must go about his task, trusting the wellsprings of his rational and intuitive faculties to make whatever judgments and assessments he will.

As to the synthetic processes that must follow, only a few words as summary are necessary. This book has constantly reiterated the necessity of synthesis as well as of analysis. Analysis is the breaking down of the total speech process into meaningful components. Synthesis is the putting together of all the diverse elements into a unified whole that has meaning, relevancy, cogency, potency, and force.

The student of criticism should not conclude that if he follows the injunctions in this book, he will then synthesize all the elements. Actually, utilizing the factors of time, place, speaker, speech, or climate of opinion is not necessary for every evaluation and criticism. Contemporary criticism is a good example.

It is true that the climate of social opinion, as indicator of changing values within a larger value system, is in a state of flux—developing and improving according to some social observers, deteriorating, or merely changing in the eyes of others. In a specific contemporary instance of political, social, intellectual, or religious speaking, the times and circumstances may need to be indicated. This would not be necessary, however, with the purely general historical background.

If one had written a critique of a contemporary political speaker, such as Hubert H. Humphrey, the Democratic vice-presidential candidate in 1964, and the critique were to be published soon after the campaign, the general historical or political milieu need not be developed at length. Perhaps it need not even be sketched in. The reason here is obvious. Most readers, if they are at all sophisticated socially and politically, would be well aware of the times and circumstances. They would read the critique within the framework of their understanding of the campaign and its political and social foundation.

The same would hold for other facets of the total critical process, not only in contemporary times, but during other periods as well. The education and family background of an orator may be of great value in a dissertation or a book length study of a speaker. However, if the critic is analyzing and assessing the use of emotional appeals in the speaking of William Miller, the Republican vice-presidential candidate in the 1964 political campaign, the delineation of familial antecedents and educational processes are not really necessary. Conversely, if the study is of William Miller's utilization of evidence and reasoning, then indicating his use of emotional reasoning may only be tangential. The student of criticism can find numerous other illustrations of the necessary use of only certain aspects of the critical dimension, depending upon the aim of the critic.

While this procedure of selecting the particular factors of criticism which will best fulfill the objective of the critic is relatively easy, other aspects of the critical process are less so. Probably most difficult is the special critical approach to be used at a particular time and to fit a critical situation most effectively. This is difficult, not so much because a unique critical theory which the critic decides to use is hard to apply (although some are obviously more complex than others, and hence make for greater problems in application), but rather that the critic himself can hardly be expected to master a dozen different theories. Few critics can approach Kenneth Burke's felicitous use, in actual critical practice, of a number of theories. Many critics are fortunate if they can master one or two of them.

Ideally speaking, the critic should make use of those elements of a particular theory which seem to fit the speech, speaker, or situation most effectively at that time. He may choose from among a number of classical, romantic, pragmatic, or contemporary formulations. The four classical ones discussed in Chapter Six—the Sophistic, Platonist, Quintilian, or Aristotelian—certainly are not the only ones at hand. Others mentioned in that chapter can also be used. Or one can select St. Augustine or Thomas Aquinas, the French theorists or the British ones, even some nineteenth century dramatic theorists and use them for rhetorical assessment. One can utilize more modern approaches—those of Kenneth Burke, or Alfred Korzybski and the general semanticists. Even quasi-literary criteria, or some contemporary dramatic hallmarks may often prove efficacious.

It has sometimes been said that the addresses of William Pitt, the Elder, the Earl of Chatham, were happy blendings of public address and theatre. On what bases has this statement been made? The public address elements may seem rather obvious, but what of the dramatic ones? It must be that the critic who originally assessed Chatham's speaking in this way used criteria of a dramatic nature, at least intrinsically, for his evaluation.

Again, the critic would not be expected to be the master of all the above formulations. But he certainly should be conversant with their salient features. He should also know how they can be used for valid assessments. Perhaps the neophyte in the art of public address criticism may attempt some exercises of his art by writing assessments using the formulations of some of the above in analyzing and evaluating some great or effective speakers. This could be done for its educational value alone, with no thought of publication. Such an exercise will not necessarily make an ideal critic who can assess within any critical medium. But it can at least help make him a functioning critic who is constantly engaged with his material and looking for new perspectives in the practice and utilization of his critical faculties.

These critical formulations should only be arbitrarily decided upon as exercises where they can be used in the same way a contemporary painter attempts to emulate Antonio Correggio or Jackson Pollock. In actual critical practice, however, the chosen approach should stem from the public address situation itself. This has been discussed in the previous chapter on interpretation and evaluation, but it cannot be stressed too much. The reference here is to the so-called inductive approach advocated by Richard McKeon and the neo-Aristotelian formulations at the University of Chicago. This approach, with rhetorical rather than literary modifications, can be of great value to the public address critic.

Simply put, the critical criteria are discerned from the work to be criticized. Then the criteria are applied to the work from which they have been discerned. It means, therefore, that the critic should follow in approach what Aristotle did in his *Rhetoric*. Contrary to much popular rhetorical opinion, the Greek master did not suggest injunctions of his own invention to be followed in every instance during his life and times and forever after. Rather he looked at the oratory of his time and found within it certain factors which made it effective (for his own time). Most oratory, he would say, dealt in an effective way with these factors he delineated. Then he put them down into his *Rhetoric*, subdividing them into speaker, speech, and audience. These theoretical formulations, it must be remembered, were basically suggested for his own times and for his own conditions.

Perhaps our own times and conditions have not quite the same standards or criteria. Certainly our own times do not give as much theoretical credence to oratory. This should make a difference in the selection of hallmarks. It is up to the critic to unearth these hallmarks, if he is to follow the inductive neo-Aristotelian approach. They should emanate from the particular work, or at least from the particular genre he is scrutinizing. Then he can use these benchmarks as measuring devices to test the efficacy of the speechmaking he is examining and analyzing. The possibilities here are limitless. But the difficulties are rather large also. Nevertheless, any critic who attempts this approach will find it challenging, intriguing, provocative, and rewarding.

The functioning critic is also enjoined to be creative. The creative aspects of public address criticism have too long been neglected. Creativity in criticism involves the two important problems of ideology and form.

Those factors dealing with content are called ideological to emphasize the importance that ideas play in public address. That they are also significant in the analytical criticism of public speaking should be apparent.

It is the wedding of creativity in speechmaking and creativity in criticism that causes some of the difficulties in the actual critiques. Just as fresh and creative speeches are not often made, so, too, fresh and creative approaches to analysis and evaluation of the ideological content of the speech are seldom forthcoming. Each critique cannot be new, fresh, sparkling, and brilliant. Nevertheless, the critic should at least attempt such an approach. It should be his ultimate goal. The student of criticism can probably profit from another perusal of the section on the interpretation and criticism of ideas in Chapter Six. Content analysis, the newer journalistic formulation, can perhaps offer some aid in the creative end of criticizing the inventive materials of a speech.

The inventive aspects are often lost sight of in critical analysis and evaluation. It must not be forgotten that the speaker does *invent* the speech. He invents it out of some kind of material, much of which originally had been invented by other speakers, thinkers, writers, publicists. Does the particular speaker under scrutiny only mouth the ideas of these others? Is his invention uniquely his own, or is it a copy of another? Ideological creativity should be present to some extent on the part of the speaker. And, of course, it should also be present, perhaps even to a larger degree, on the part of the critic. His is the role of ascertaining the facets of invention and discerning their consequences. While speakers are often imitative and derivative, critics should avoid these hazards and try for uniqueness and singularity.

Possibly what this means on the part of the critic is the development of a kind of sixth sense to tell him that this particular address or this speaker has weight, is worth the time of a scrupulous analysis. The mediocre little speeches, like mediocre little inventions, keep whistling the same tune. They are not worthy of analysis just as many inventions are not even worthy of patents, much less of being used to aid society.

Unfortunately, in the heat of a political campaign, a social issue, or a religious crusade, the worthiness of the speechmaking is often deemed greater than it really is. Too often, from the standpoint of invention, the same themes are played in the same way.

Consider a political campaign. It is not so much that Goldwater or Johnson were saying the same thing time and time again. This is somewhat understandable. They may be confronting different audiences; or even with similar audiences, repetition is a valid and valuable rhetorical device. But ideological creativity demands at least that the substantiation and the discernment should come not from the same sources all the time. While it is true, to some extent, that everything has been said and done before, it has not all been said and done in the same manner.

Moreover, the lesser political lights are generally a good deal worse. A gubernatorial or senatorial campaign may be interesting, rhetorically as well as politically, and not only from a regional point of view. A Rockefeller or a Fulbright can often bring more significant ideological and rhetorical facets into a campaign than politicians who campaign on a national scale.

Or consider a social issue such as racial equality, about which a great amount of speechmaking has been done. Does the speaker, as ideologist, bring to his invention the same old tired clichés used by orators, past or present? Or will he attempt to draw on fresh perspectives, new and different authorities, interesting analogues, fresh evidence, and exemplary and cogent reasoning? Part of the force and power of the new egalitarian revolution in which Negro and white have been playing such a significant role has come about because of the inventive skill of speakers, such as Dr. Martin Luther King. Does the public address critic, in his study, discern this? Does he furthermore invent his critique out of fresher, brighter, more newly minted materials, materials that are analogous in inventive perception to that of the speaker?

Consider a religious crusade. Religion has existed since time immemorial. What can be freshly creative about religious speaking? Or, for that matter, what can be freshly creative about the criticism of that speaking? This is up to the critic whose concern is with religious speaking. Perhaps the neighborhood minister, priest, or rabbi does not offer creative insights, ideologically. But perhaps a Reinhold Niebuhr, a John Cogley, or a Will Herberg might. Why is it that these important theologians of different religious persuasions manage to do so? Probably because, ideologically, they constantly search for new materials for their lectures and addresses. In their invention, they go to contemporary findings in philosophy, literature, political theory, social theory, political practice, and social practice. They search constantly for new relationships among these seemingly diverse elements in order to discover new and fresh perceptions. And their speeches show it. The old theologies are not merely refurbished in the process. Some of them are literally given new life. It is not enough for the critic of public address to discover these unique elements in political, social, or religious speechmaking. He must discern these characteristics and add his own ideological perceptions, his own discoveries of the new relationships from the speaker's relationships. This is the problem of ideological creativity which the critic faces. This is the difficulty he must overcome, whatever kind of speaking is his main concern.

The problem of ideological creativity is not the only one. There is the further problem of formal creativity. Here, too, the difficulty is two-fold: from the standpoint of the speaker, and from the standpoint of the critic.

A speech becomes great not only because of the ideological commitment it contains, but also because of its formal characteristics—the fashion in which it is couched. In speechmaking, sometimes ideas predominate; sometimes form does. With form, as with ideas, the critical analyst must separate the wheat from the chaff. Most speeches probably have very little value if the criteria for judgment are the unique, creative, formal factors which they contain. Very few speeches are highly creative from the formal viewpoint. Many are different; some are somewhat new; but few are really original and creative.

If this is so, then the critic must first rapidly examine a speech to see if it is truly unique or original. Then he must settle down to wrestle with it in a more detailed fashion for the purpose of analytical evaluation. He must discern what element or elements of form—arrangement, style, juxtaposition of appeals, perhaps delivery, or any of the other multitudinous facets of form—give the speech its unique flavor. He must ascertain further how these creative formal elements work to fortify the creative ideological ones.

It is not enough for the critic of public address to have this discerning eye, ear, and mind. He must develop his own formal creativity. After all, if his rational and intuitive faculties provide him with the perceptions to unearth these factors, they should also aid him in communicating these in an effective and original formal manner. The great critic is not the one who merely has the perceptions and the insights, but he is the one who also can communicate them creatively. This faculty is most important, if one wants or needs to differentiate among the various critical faculties. Actually, however, all of these have their unique qualities; all add to the total critical picture.

If there is one detriment to effective public address criticism, if there is one important reason why it is not cherished more or, perhaps, even read, it is that much of it is dry, pedantic, undisciplined, undistinguished. The academic style prevails. And while academicians may not be loath to wade through a study in order to get whatever discernments are present in the critique, most lay readers hesitate to do so. The latter prefer sparkling, insightful assessments, even controversial ones, rather than phlegmatic, laconic ones. Perhaps the only injunction that can be given to the public address critic is to read other kinds of critical writing—art, drama, literature, music. He should look at these studies in the respective professional publications, as well as in more popular journals such as *Atlantic, Harper's Magazine, The Reporter, The National Review,* or *Modern Age.* Much of the evaluative writing in the latter magazines is not only reputable from the scholarly viewpoint, but intriguing from the artistic one.

Again the theory here is not that the public address critic emulate these completely. How could he? It is rather that the very reading can aid him in subtle ways to enhance and develop his own style, to make it more readable for the lay reader. This is not to suggest that the critic take completely to heart the recent injunctions on the art of plain talk such as those of Rudolf Flesch. While it is true that some criticism might profit from a simpler, more conversational idiom, much of it would not. Complex ideas articulated in a complex manner by a sophisticated critical writer often need a more elaborate style than simple ideas mouthed by a simplistic critic. To suggest that any speech, be it that of a humorist, an eminent intellectual, or an abstract theologian should be treated formally in the same simple manner by the public address critic, would be poor advice indeed. The opposite injunction would not make complete sense, either. To suggest that each speech be analyzed critically in the formal idiom of the particular speaker would produce imitation and lack of insight. The true artist in criticism uses various tools in different situations. Synthesis is always best in criticism.

There is little doubt that a spare as well as an elegant style can be part of a particular critique. To emphasize always the spare aspects at the expense of the more elaborate ones in some way yields simple rather than cogent thinking. It is true that the critic may at times need to explain difficult passages, to interpret them for the reader, and to use the historical exegesis or poetical explication in the process. This may simplify some ideas; but the critic, like the speaker, has explication and simplification as only one of his main objectives. If his critiques are to be worthwhile, they must be artistic and persuasive.

If one is to utilize some of the significant views of the classicists for criticism, one could agree here with both Cicero and Aristotle. Cicero's persistent urgings that in a speech the formal elements—especially style—should be appropriate to occasion and appropriate from the point of view of being neither overly sparse, or overly elegant, could be applied as well to the writing of speech criticism. So, too, with Aristotle. His aphorism of the "Golden Mean," coming from his *Nichomachian Ethics,* could be applied by the critic. It emphasizes moderation through the ideal of doing nothing to excess. This may not always be appropriate since a more extreme point of view may have merit when dealing with an extreme speech. But even here, a moderate tone—and this is part of both the formal and ideational elements—which synthesizes the spare and elegant may very well have the most persuasive impact.

For it must be remembered that it is not only the orator who uses the rhetoric of persuasion. While it is true that the critic relies on a rational delineation of truth in the assessment of a particular speech, this by itself is not sufficient. Just as the orator need energize and discover truth together with the audience, so should the critic. Therefore, the critic should apply in his criticism those rhetorical and social elements he so ably dissects in the speaker.

Any theory of public address criticism that the critic follows is a theory of value. This is so because the critic constantly sets up standards which are significant and important to him as a theorist. Then the application of these measuring devices must be accomplished in such a manner as to convince others of two factors. The first is that the theoretical formulations used for the evaluation are apt, correct, and the most valuable ones that can be used at that time and with the particular work. The second is to convince the reader that the assessment, which uses the particular formulations, does get at some germ of truth about the orator and his work. For this truth is necessary. For this rhetoric is necessary. For this persuasion is necessary.

SELECTED BIBLIOGRAPHY

Black, Edwin, *Rhetorical Criticism*, New York: Macmillan, 1965.

Burke, Kenneth, *A Grammar of Motives*, New York: Prentice-Hall, 1952.

———, *A Rhetoric of Motives*, New York: Prentice-Hall, 1953.

Hillbruner, Anthony, "Creativity in Contemporary Criticism," *Western Speech*, XXIV, 1 (Winter, 1960), 5–11.

———, "Criticism as Persuasion," *Southern Speech Journal,* XXVIII, 4 (Summer, 1963), 260–267.

Koestler, Arthur, *The Act of Creation,* New York: Macmillan, 1964.

McKeon, Richard, "Rhetoric and Poetic in the Philosophy of Aristotle." *Aristotle's Poetics and English Literature,* Elder Olson, ed., Chicago: The University of Chicago Press, 1965, pp. 201–236.

Index

Index